Sold Out Forever

101 Essential Items to Grab Before the U.S. Dollar Vanishes

by

Damian Brindle

Sold Out Forever: 101 Essential Items to Grab Before the U.S. Dollar Vanishes

Published by Great Books, LLC

P.O. Box 1157

Liberty, MO. 64069

Copyright © 2022 Great Books, LLC

Visit the author's website at https://rethinksurvival.com

Printed in U.S.A.

ISBN: 9798354048977

First Edition

Disclaimer

Table of Contents

Introduction

As I write this, during late summer of 2022, the United States is experiencing record inflation, the likes of which have not been seen in over forty years. Some argue inflation is as bad as it was during the last World War over seventy-five years ago, while others suggest that our current inflationary troubles are merely transitory. I argue this is only the beginning.

For starters, the price of food continues to rise, in part because of ever-increasing fertilizer and diesel costs, but also due to supply chain issues and even global unrest. Widespread food scarcity, particularly in the least developed nations, is anticipated to strike America next spring. I don't know the exact timing, but I know my grocery bill keeps rising. I suspect yours is as well.

Furthermore, the domestic economy continues to falter, which only hastens our decline, and that's to say nothing of our government's continued and unrestrained printing of money to put it off for as long as possible. At some point, our fiscal policy choices will become unavoidable, and it will be you and I left holding the bag. Sadly, we may already be too late.

Let me ask you this: What will you do if the price of your groceries doubles or triples within only a few months? How will you feed your family if store shelves are nearly empty because of continued supply chain shortages? And what happens when the unprepared masses finally panic after realizing the truth? Nothing good, I can assure you of that.

Undoubtedly, the price of your groceries is only one of many concerns when inflation truly hits us. We'll discuss everything you need to know in due course, but for now, realize that America is headed for a sharp decline over the next few years, and likely a complete ousting as world leader once the U.S. petrodollar ceases to exist. How quickly and how bad our decline will be remains to be seen; geopolitics are rather complex, after all. I can say, however, that what's coming is likely unavoidable. It's time for you to prepare yourself and your family while the U.S. dollar still holds some value.

Let me be clear: I'm not saying you should empty your bank accounts after reading this and buy everything I suggest immediately. That would be irresponsible of you and of me. Rather, I suggest you prioritize use of any disposable income to focus on purchasing more of the items which I outline rather than on, say, another smartphone, bigger television, or a new car when your old ones likely still function fine. Odds are good that none of these modern wants are truly necessary, though more food, clothing, tools, as well as many other essential items will be.

It's time for you to prepare yourself and your family while the U.S. dollar still holds some value.

How This Book is Organized

I organized this book into two main parts: items you should purchase to see you through the initial crisis, and items to help you survive until society stabilizes.

To keep this easy to read, I'll introduce a new item to discuss every few pages. But I also want this to be a useful guide, rather than merely a list of things to buy, so I'll discuss why these specific items are useful to you, how much to purchase, as well as alternative options and supplemental ideas where appropriate.

About Website Links

This was originally written to be an electronic book only with many website links referenced throughout. Because this is a paperback book, however, referencing these links can be tedious if you had to type them into your web browser by hand. To make this process easier on you, I have consolidated all referenced links into a single resource here: **https://rethinksurvival.com/books/sold-out-links.html**.

For completeness, however, all referenced links will also be included in Appendix E.

Grab Your Free 101-Point Checklist

Odds are that you won't remember everything discussed when you're finished reading this book. To make your life easier, I've created a free, easy-to-reference, 101-point checklist you can download that outlines everything discussed. You'll find a link to it here so that you can follow along if you like and at the end of this book in Appendix A, but please do read the entire book first. Download your free, easy-to-reference survival items checklist here.[1]

Last, I reference many specific products throughout. You may either search for them directly on Amazon, or you can find direct links to them on the book's recommendations page.[2]

Part 1: Items to Buy Now to See You Through the Initial Crisis

The items highlighted in part one are chosen to act as a bridge during the ensuring chaos, for when the unprepared masses wake up. They're intended to keep you one step ahead of an angry crowd that will inevitably panic buy. Stores will become a frenzied mess for months to come, supply chain disruptions will follow (or lead), and governments at all levels will intervene (possibly with some short-lived success), but none of it will stop the landslide that is inflation.

The good news is that most of the items discussed in part one are those that you will use up at some point. Most things won't go bad for many years to come. And if we assume that prices for these goods will continue to rise or remain stagnant, then there's little harm in purchasing more now. Personally, I don't see the cost of food becoming less expensive. The cost of paper goods, personal hygiene supplies, and cleaners aren't coming down either. I can say the same for nearly everything on this list. That should speak volumes.

Last, while I believe all items presented in part one are essential to stock up on, if you must focus, then start at the beginning and work your way down. Let's get started.

Shelf-Stable Foods

We all instinctively understand how crucial food is to our survival. It's why people often resort to taking desperate measures when they're starving, such as by consuming clearly rancid or spoiled food, tempting fate by trying unknown wild edibles, and even eating dirt or sand to stave off their hunger pangs.

Without enough calories, our bodies will eventually waste away to nothing. Without adequate nutrition, we're susceptible to an assortment of otherwise preventable ailments. And without proper food storage methods, such as refrigeration and canning, the wide variety of fresh food we rely on to survive is vulnerable to spoilage, which only increases our chances of developing further illnesses.

Although modern agricultural practices, sprawling transportation networks, and food handling procedures have done a wonderful job of minimizing the aforementioned problems, they also afford us a false sense of security because we no longer appreciate just how fragile our food supply chain truly is, particularly if there's ever a major hiccup in the system. As I see it, there are fewer greater domestic concerns than being truly unable to feed citizens.

As the cost of our basic foodstuffs—wheat, sugar, soybeans—rises because of inflation and other pressures, we will see unprecedented food shortages, price gouging, rationing, and even theft. Now is the time to buy food to act as a bridge between whatever is to come and an eventual return to normalcy.

Which Foods to Purchase

The short answer is that you should focus on purchasing any shelf-stable foods that your family regularly consumes. This would likely include an assortment of canned goods, such as canned meats, beans, vegetables, and fruits. Almost anything that doesn't need refrigeration, like spaghetti and pasta sauce, dehydrated potatoes, packaged side dishes, and even boxes of cereals, are all good to incorporate. If you want to make your life even easier, add ready-to-eat foods, such as canned soups, chili, and boxes of macaroni and cheese, to name a few options.

Remember that babies and pets need unique food, too. Most dry pet food—and even many canned foods—will last for several months if not years unopened. Most powdered, unopened baby formula should last a year or longer if stored in a cool, dry place, but always check expiration dates before use. And if you have young children, then stock up on their favorites because they can often be the pickiest people of all.

How Much Food to Purchase

Understand that these shelf-stable foods aren't intended to be your only means of sustenance for months on end. Hence, I'm not expecting you to purchase a year's worth of canned food right now. Rather, shelf-stable foods, such as those mentioned previously, should fill in the gaps as the cost of the grocery store foods you purchase regularly continues to rise. At some point, we should expect things to level out and return to some normalcy—even if it means significant government intervention via rationing—but who knows how long that could be. My guess is a year or two.

Realize, too, that you could also have unexpected mouths to feed, such as family members or friends who move in. Of course, whether you choose to be so generous is up to you, but whether by choice or by circumstance, it's a genuine possibility.

Ultimately, I suggest you purchase enough shelf-stable foods to feed your current household for a minimum of three to six months solely from what you have stored. Remember, however, that their purpose is to supplement whatever foods you can purchase until the country straightens out, which, assuming things don't go completely haywire, should stretch your food resources for the better part of a year.

Exactly how much is three to six months of food? That's difficult to pin down, especially if you purchase a variety of fresh foods regularly. That number will also largely depend on how many people are in your family, how much food people eat—teenagers eat more than adults—and whether the food you store is calorie-dense. While a food storage calculator or calorie calculator may come in handy, odds are that you already have some idea of how much shelf-stable versus fresh food you consume.[3,4] Do some math, then take an educated guess as to how much shelf-stable food you'll need to buy to equal three to six months. And even if you over-buy, that's fine.

If you'd like to stockpile more food, then do so. But if your financial resources are limited, as are mine, realize that food is only one of many areas that deserve your focus.

Going Beyond the Basic Foodstuffs

If you want to take your food storage to the next level, I suggest you buy bulk foods, but with two caveats:

1. You need the ability to process some bulk foods. As an example, you can purchase all the bulk wheat that you want, but if you don't have a quality grain grinder, then having wheat on hand will do you little good since most people only ever transform wheat into flour for baking.

13

2. You should have experience using bulk food in meals. For instance, cooking with dry beans is nothing like opening a can of beans you're accustomed to purchasing from the store. It requires a lot more time, energy, and water to make them edible than most folks realize.

With that in mind, there are nearly a dozen bulk foods which I encourage people to purchase when they're ready. I prefer to purchase these specific bulk foods from a nearby LDS Home Storage Center for cost and convenience reasons, though it is possible to find most of the bulk foods I recommend at a local warehouse store, such as Costco or Sam's Club.[5]

For this discussion, I'll suggest you focus on the easiest to use bulk foods, specifically rice, oats, spaghetti, macaroni, and pancake mix, although the pancake mix could spoil over time due to mold growth. Packaged dry beans are fine to include, too, but they don't last for years either, especially if not properly packaged, and even then dry beans can remain hard no matter how long they've been cooked. Last, I would only recommend you store wheat if you have a quality grain grinder, as mentioned previously, along with everything required to make bread—the most likely purpose for storing wheat—from scratch, such as plenty of salt, sugar, oil, and yeast. For what it's worth, I prefer honey over sugar in most instances because it is more nutritious and stores nearly forever.

There are plenty more shelf-stable foods you can store, specifically foods which maximize your health during hard times. I wrote a book about the topic if you're interested, but so long as you focus on stockpiling a wide variety of shelf-stable foods, then you're on the right track.[6] I'll include the complete food storage checklist in Appendix B.

Although I prefer my local LDS Home Storage Center, I realize you may not have one close by. Instead, shop at your local warehouse stores, such as Costco or Sam's Club, to purchase as much food as you can in bulk. If you're not a member of these clubs, try a discount grocery store, like Aldi's or Save-A-Lot. Barring these options, do the best you can at Walmart or shop sales at your local grocery store.

How to Store Food Safely

The biggest concerns with long-term food storage are exposure to heat, humidity, oxygen, light, and to a lesser extent, rodent or insect infestation. There are other potential problems, such as spoilage or food degradation, but I'll ignore those for now because they're largely controlled by exposure to heat and humidity. The good news is that canned foods tend not to suffer from problems with oxygen, light, or infestations because of how they're packaged. Many shelf-stable boxed foods, such as instant potatoes, don't suffer from oxygen or light penetration, though rodents and insects can be a concern.

About the only problem every shelf-stable food will have is exposure to hot or cold temperatures, and to a lesser extent humidity. Heat is a serious problem because it directly affects the food's nutritional content, flavor, appearance, and even texture. Ideally, you'll want to store all food at 75 degrees Fahrenheit or cooler, and in as dry of an environment as possible. Basements are great; attics, not so much.

Allowing canned foods to freeze may be equally problematic, as this online article points out: "When water freezes, it expands, causing the airtight seal of the can to be compromised. Once the seal breaks, the food is exposed to the air, allowing bacteria to grow. The bacteria can cause foodborne illnesses and cause symptoms such as diarrhea, vomiting, and fever."[7]

Never store food—even bulk food—in an attic or non-air-conditioned garage or shed. You'll avoid getting sick and minimize food degradation concerns. You'll also be more aware of budding problems, such as ants getting into your honey, or a can of tomato sauce that's unexpectedly bulging.

Where to Store Food

I've seen people store food, especially canned goods, in a variety of creative ways. For example, I've seen folks raise their beds or couches and stash canned food underneath. I've seen people move furniture away from walls and stash cans there. People have turned food storage buckets into table legs. They'll buy or build racks and store food on the backs of doors, next to their refrigerator, and use up every inch of pantry wall space. If you have little room, creativity is the mother of all inventions.

If you have extra space—because it's not as efficient as merely stacking cans one atop another—consider a commercially made pantry can organizer.

The Shelf Reliance Pantry Can Organizer expands horizontally, adjusts to can height, and is stackable.[8] They're perfect for most pantries and ensure you're always using the oldest cans first. If you prefer a different option, just search on Amazon for *pantry can organizer* and you'll find plenty of alternatives.

For those who want to get more serious about their canned food storage, consider larger storage racks.

We've used the Harvest 72 by Shelf Reliance (shown above) for years, though I believe it's discontinued. If interested, I found a similar large can rack, sold by ThriveLife.com, but it appears designed to only work with their specific cans of food.[9] For the price, I would call and ask before outright purchasing one.

18

Of course, you don't have to go to such extremes. You don't have to move furniture or buy an expensive can rack. You could simply stack cans until your shelves bulge and hope for the best. But it's always best to use your oldest food first, so I encourage you to have some system in place, even if it's nothing more than moving the old cans out and placing the new cans in behind.

Alternatives and Supplements

Seasonings and spices are crucial to engaging a bored palate, particularly if you're forced to cook more often with bland foods. Although unlikely if you choose to stockpile a variety of shelf-stable foods, appetite fatigue—deliberately choosing not to eat because of a lack of interest in food—is still a concern, primarily with children. An assortment of seasonings and spices are always welcome in the kitchen, and because most spices will last for many years without concern, I encourage you to stock up.

Start with purchasing plenty of salt because it's necessary to sustain life, though I would also include other common spices, such as pepper, cumin, chili powder, garlic powder, onion powder, and oregano, to name several of the most common ones. Or just buy plenty more of whatever spices it is that you use regularly, and if you're concerned about their longevity, pack them in a vacuum-sealed bag, and store out of sunlight and away from heat. Discount stores, such as the Dollar Tree, are good places to get seasonings inexpensively. You might also consider growing your own. It's not terribly hard, and many grown both indoors and out.

Supplemental activities include gardening, hunting, trapping, canning, pickling, fermenting, dehydrating, and freeze-drying. If one or more of these activities appear interesting, then I strongly encourage you to get started now, because trying to accomplish any of the above after the dollar crashes is likely too late, not to mention possibly dangerous if you get it wrong.

Gardening, for instance, is wonderful, but it takes a lot of time—both in daily maintenance and waiting for a payoff of food to eat—as well as the right materials, like vegetable seeds, soil mix, gardening tools, and plenty more. Perhaps more important is the experience of knowing what to grow where you live, when to plant, and how to deal with problems, such as wildlife and bugs, all of which will pose complications you shouldn't be attempting to figure out for the first time during hard times. And I haven't even mentioned the problem of what to do with the inevitable excess you'll reap if all goes well. Gardening isn't easy, fast, or for the faint of heart.

Hunting can be dangerous to you and others if you're inexperienced, and then there's knowing how to process game properly. If you absolutely must have meat for dinner, but you have no clue how to hunt, find a mentor and learn while you still can, or find someone who does hunt and work out a trade deal.

Canning, pickling, dehydrating, and freeze-drying all have their pros and cons, which I won't get into here. I will say that whatever options you choose to further your food storage goals will become more difficult as time goes on, and may even become impossible as prices rise and scarcity becomes the norm.

A quality multivitamin would be another healthy item to stock up on now. Although we're trying our best to include a wide range of food, and thus a variety of nutrients, we should cover our bases. Purchase, at minimum, a shelf-stable multivitamin for each member of the household. Wholesale clubs sell large bottles for relatively inexpensive prices, or search online. Individual vitamins might be of use, too. Vitamin C, in particular, is good to consider because of how much it does for the body. Vitamin D might be useful, too, though you're usually better off getting what you need from sunlight, in moderate doses, of course. Last, electrolyte powder may come in handy during times of stress, exertion, or illness, such as dehydration caused by diarrhea.

Food is crucial to your health and survival, and it's still relatively inexpensive. Start stockpiling now.

Hygiene and Cleaning Supplies

Keeping yourself and your environment clean will become even more crucial than normal during hard times if we assume that (1) your nutritional intake may be lacking because of lesser availability of quality food—notably fruits, vegetables, meat, and dairy—and (2) there will be a general erosion of the country's medical system as inflation causes even routine healthcare, such as a doctor's visit, to be sought only in the most dire of circumstances. The average American will put off their health concerns in favor of putting food on the table or keeping a roof over their head. We can expect a similar level of going without of any standard first-world luxury, including air conditioning, clean water, and entertainment.

With this assumption in mind, I firmly believe in gathering plenty of the following supplies, many of which you will probably use down the road no matter what happens. But I realize that such a list can become very long indeed, so I won't attempt to include every personal hygiene and cleaning supply you could purchase. Rather, the following suggestions are only intended to get you thinking about those items that are most likely to be used by the average family, including:

- Personal hygiene supplies, such as plenty of hand soap, bar soap, shampoo, conditioner, deodorant, toothpaste, floss, mouthwash, feminine hygiene products, shaving supplies, lotion, and hand sanitizer.

- Assorted household cleaners, including dish soap (Dawn dish soap, specifically, goes a long way and has many additional uses), laundry soap, bathroom cleaners, floor and carpet cleaners, spray disinfectants, and wet wipes.
- Toilet paper, facial tissue, paper towels, and napkins.
- Garbage bags (both 13-gallon kitchen bags and 30-gallon or larger bags).
- Sunscreen, bug spray.
- Additional supplies, such as isopropyl alcohol, hydrogen peroxide, bleach, white vinegar, baking soda, borax, and ammonia, to name a handful of supplies we keep on hand.
- Supplies for children and infants, like diapers or pull-ups, while bearing in mind that they will quickly grow into larger sizes.

Undoubtedly, the list of items you rely on will differ depending on your specific needs, though the above list is a good place to start. Regardless, I'm positive there are many supplies that you make use of which you'll regret not having if they're unavailable or become too expensive to purchase down the road. Start making that list now and then stock up.

How Much to Purchase

It should go without saying that not all hygiene items are of equal importance. Surely, having more shaving supplies on hand than soap, or including more deodorant than toothpaste, would be silly for your health. In addition, adjust quantities based on future expectations. For instance, you may not spend much time outside right now, but that may change. Thus, having a few bottles of sunscreen around may be of use if you expect to be outside more than usual.

Of course, only you will know how much of these items you use regularly. And, as with food, it never hurts to have more on hand for a variety of reasons, even because of extra people in the house. Unlike foodstuffs, I encourage you to purchase a year's worth of these supplies, in part because of their relative usefulness to your health, but also buying in bulk will save a lot of money. Write dates on bottoms of cans or keep a spreadsheet or other tally list if you need help to determine how much you actually use.

If you must prioritize, focus on bar soap, hand soap (if you prefer liquid soaps), toothpaste and floss, feminine hygiene products, and liquid dish soap. I would also stock up on toilet paper—we all know how quickly toilet paper disappears after the great shortage of 2020.

It would also be a good idea to stockpile several bottles or boxes of the basic ingredients mentioned previously—white vinegar, baking soda, isopropyl alcohol, and so—as well, but only if you intend on making your own cleaners and personal hygiene supplies at some point, which we'll discuss briefly. Bleach is also useful to have on hand, both as a cleaner and as a temporary water treatment option, but it loses efficacy over time, even if unopened, so don't expect it to be viable for many years to come.

The Problems With Stockpiling Supplies

While it's relatively easy and inexpensive right now to gather many of the items you already make use of daily, begin planning beyond merely stockpiling such supplies because, although you can easily purchase years' worth of personal hygiene supplies and household cleaners, I can tell you from personal experience that this isn't always the best plan.

For starters, it's easy to misplace supplies. As I write this, we're over a year past moving back to the Midwest, and I can tell you that several times during our packing, I found supplies of all sorts stashed in places that I'd completely forgotten about. Regrettably, some of those stashed supplies were no longer viable solely because of my neglect.

Another major problem is that years inevitably turn into decades at some point. I've been prepping long enough now that I've run into supplies which are far beyond their expiration date because I'd held on to them for so long. Worse, some of these supplies are assuredly less trustworthy simply because I'd exposed them to extreme temperatures by storing them in a non-air-conditioned garage for years. I get lazy, too.

Alternatives and Supplements

You could be better off storing the raw materials to make many of the aforementioned hygiene and cleaning supplies because the raw materials typically last longer, are less expensive, aren't as affected by temperature extremes and neglect, and are often as effective as their pre-made equivalents.

The best part is that we can make most household cleaners with only a handful of basic materials, like white vinegar, baking soda, borax, and Epsom Salts. Add in a few additional supplies, such as isopropyl alcohol, coconut oil, and cornstarch, and you can make almost any cleaner or hygiene product.

Of course, you'll need to know how to make it all, so I recommend you print out your favorite recipes from online resources or purchase a book.[10] Realize, too, that you can make an assortment of natural hygiene and cleaning products using essential oils, or herbs if you prefer an organic approach. Stock up on what you're accustomed to buying to see you through, then add in the basic ingredients for hard times.

First Aid Supplies and Medications

Have you heard that eighty or ninety percent of pharmaceuticals used domestically are produced in China? The implication is that if we ever ceased trade with China for whatever reason, then we would be in terrible trouble. It's not true that China makes most of our medications, but we do source a variety of pharmaceuticals from around the world, including from China, India, and the European Union as the three primary sources outside of the United States.[11]

What I can say is that if we ever have another significant problem with the global supply chain, or if the cost of manufacturing and transporting pharmaceuticals becomes truly cost-prohibitive as global inflation takes hold, expect most first aid, over-the-counter and prescription medications to be worth their weight in gold.

Thankfully, you can still purchase first aid supplies and over-the-counter medications at dirt-cheap prices right now. Stop by your local warehouse club or grocery store and purchase whatever you're missing, even if you don't expect to use it soon.

Start with basic wound care supplies, such as antibiotic ointment, a wide variety of bandages, plenty of sterile gauze pads and rolls, medical tape, elastic wrap, moleskin, and latex-free gloves.

Include analgesics (pain medications), decongestants, antihistamines, antacids, antidiarrheals, laxatives, expectorants, topical analgesics, and topical steroids.

If you must prioritize the list above, focus primarily on medications to help with respiratory issues and wound care, since they are often the most troubling.

Luckily, many over-the-counter medications will last much longer than their expiration date.[12] There are exceptions, such as with some liquid medications, along with storage concerns, like being subject to extreme heat or humidity, but if you store your first aid supplies and medications in climate-controlled conditions, then they'll last that much longer.

Prescription medications are a much bigger problem many of us will face. Truth be told, they're so heavily regulated by insurance companies that it will be difficult to buy a significant stockpile of anything. Perhaps the only honest solution I can offer is to discuss your concerns with a doctor and see if they'd be willing to write you a lengthier prescription or maybe prescribe a less expensive, often generic, alternative which might then be purchased without going through insurance. If they're unwilling, then consider looking for a different physician. I know this isn't ideal, but if you or a family member rely upon essential pharmaceuticals, it's best to decide now what you'll do should worse come to worst.

How Much to Purchase

The good news is that you probably don't have to purchase a lot of many medications. For example, a large bottle of Ibuprofen, Tylenol, or even Benadryl should last you for years. In addition, you likely won't need much of many over-the-counter medications, especially anti-diarrheal, laxatives, or antacids, since the problems they ease are usually temporary. Expectorants and decongestants fall somewhere in between only needing a little and wanting plenty on hand. Again, if you shop at a wholesaler, like Costco or Sam's Club, they're about as economical of a price as you can find for over-the-counter medications.

Other items, specifically those for wound care, can be used up quickly when dealing with significant trauma. Gauze pads and rolls, and to a lesser extent disposable gloves, should be purchased in bulk.

I'm not a doctor or healthcare practitioner, so take my advice with a very large grain of salt. Better yet, reach out to a physician and seek their advice on such matters. Another option is to buy a good medical preparedness book. *The Survival Medicine Handbook* by Dr. Joseph Alton is a superb choice.[13] The *Prepper's Medical Handbook* by William Forgey is another one I recommend.[14]

Should You Stockpile Antibiotics?

If you're unable to receive proper medical care for a significant length of time, then fish antibiotics might be your last resort.[15] If you're going to stockpile them for such a purpose, then I recommend you get the Pocket Drug Guide for Nurses, or a similar book so that you'll understand proper dosages, interactions, cautions, and so forth.[16]

I must point out, however, that the FDA does not approve fish antibiotics for human consumption. Worse, you might actually cause more harm than good if you're dealing with a viral infection or using the wrong antibiotic simply because you didn't know any better.[17] That could be catastrophic.

It's also illegal to purchase antibiotics from overseas or to purchase them online without a doctor's prescription, though there are online services that may be of interest, though I've never tried them.[18] It's also possible that your pharmacist can offer helpful solutions beyond what I'm aware of.

My advice is to never take chances with your health, even during troubled times. Always seek proper medical advice and stay within the law. With that in mind, there's no harm in locating a nearby neighbor who has medical knowledge and reach out. And if you can offer something in return, then all the better.

Alternatives and Supplements

There are many potential, natural alternatives to basic over-the-counter medications, including herbs, essential oils, and a variety of tinctures. In fact, many people in my life prefer more natural alternatives to pharmaceuticals these days. But you must be careful with their use because, although herbal supplements, for instance, are usually regulated by the FDA, they aren't scrutinized to the degree that pharmaceuticals are. "Herbal products — including those labeled as 'natural' — can have strong effects in the body," as this Mayo Clinic article points out.[19] I can say the same for any so-called natural product. Personally, I see little harm in exploring alternatives, so long as your primary care physician is in the loop and can monitor for unwanted side effects.

Appropriate Clothing and Shoes

How many outfits do you have? What about pairs of shoes? Maybe your closet is arranged by seasons, you have an assortment of outfits for parties and work, and your shoes match every occasion. But would any of your attire be truly useful if you needed it for survival? How long would any of your clothing last if you couldn't wash it regularly or, worse, if you had to wash it by hand? Would your shoes be useful if you had to work outside day in and day out? Would any of your clothing or shoe choices keep your feet warm in freezing weather, or is it mostly to look good?

There is one benefit to having a wide variety of clothes—not needing to wash laundry for months if push came to shove. But aside from this minor benefit, I'm willing to bet that most clothing you own would be relatively useless if you had to rely on it for anything other than moving from one sheltered area to another. Sadly, most clothing purchased these days isn't made to truly last or keep you safe from harsh weather, but you can do better.

When I talk about outdoor clothing, I'm usually thinking about staying warm and dry in cold weather, so we'll start there. You'll want to have a quality windbreaker and insulated jacket to start with. Remember to include insulated gloves, thick socks, and a stocking cap, too. A pair of insulated underwear couldn't hurt either, but how warm you need to stay will depend on your climate. Purchase insulated boots, such as snow boots, though a good pair of hiking boots should suffice for use around the house and double as bug out shoes should the need arise. There's also no harm in having extra sweatshirts to act as an intermediate layer of insulation, underclothes—particularly socks and underwear—because they wear out faster than other clothing, and a variety of rugged gloves because you may end up wearing them day and night if you're unable to keep your house warm.

Again, how aggressively you'll want to get will depend on your climate. As an example, when we used to live in less-than-sunny Seattle, a decent rain jacket and insulating layer would've sufficed in even the coldest months, but now that we've moved back to the Midwest, a much warmer coat is in order, not to mention better boots, gloves, and hats. A quality rain jacket and rubber boots never hurts to keep around.

When it's hot outside, you may wrongly assume that all you need is a pair of shorts, t-shirt, and sandals. Why is this thinking wrong? Because when the dollar collapses, and you find it's too expensive to cool your home—or there are rolling brownouts—you'll no longer be transitioning from one air-conditioned environment to another, such as from your house to a car, but you may now spend a majority of your time in a consistently hot, muggy and miserable environment, which is precisely the environment many bugs enjoy. To keep them from irritating you nonstop, I suggest you purchase lightweight, breathable clothing that covers your extremities, including long-sleeved shirts and pants. I know this goes against what most people expect, but you will thank me when it helps to keep the bugs at bay and reduces unnecessary sun exposure. Even so, there's no harm in ensuring you have plenty of shorts and t-shirts for those times when bugs aren't such a problem and you can stay inside.

Quality shoes and boots are equally important as outdoor clothing for a variety of reasons. Not only can the right shoes keep your feet warm in the bitter cold, but they keep your feet and socks dry, help keep you safe from being wounded if you step on the wrong thing, can keep you from twisting an ankle given the right support, and make it easier to maneuver over a wide variety of terrain while performing many tasks.

Put another way: If you believe your loafers, high heels, or even sneakers will be of much use when shoes become impossible to purchase, you're sadly mistaken. Most shoes break down quickly with any actual use, won't really keep your feet warm or dry, and could become a hazard in the wrong situation.

Buy quality hiking boots, work boots, or Army boots, any of which are much better alternatives. No doubt quality shoes will be more expensive when purchased new, and are often difficult to find second-hand. Keeping an old pair of sneakers around is better than nothing, even if only worn around the inside of your home. And if you're considering tossing out old shoes, hang on to them just in case you need something down the road or if growing children or other people, such as family or friends, do.

Although it will take more effort, I suggest initially shopping at local thrift stores, such as Goodwill, if you don't currently have any useful clothing or shoes. If you can shop near the end of winter, in particular, you'll often find an assortment of useful, yet inexpensive, clothing that most people will glance over. That said, there may not be time to wait until next winter, so if you're missing something crucial, such as a quality coat or boots, then it may be best to get them now.

Let's not forget those of us who have growing kids. Do you have enough clothing and shoes that they can grow into for years to come? Remember that kids grow fast—even through their teenage years—which means they may quickly outgrow what you expect them to use even within the course of a year. Scour secondhand stores for deals or, better yet, local online swap and shop groups, and then stock up as

35

much as is reasonable. Search Facebook for thrift groups, as there are often many of them to choose from. You might even post "wanted" ads in these groups and get clothing for free, but always follow moderator rules or risk being banned outright.

One final thought on clothing choices. Some folks suggest purchasing clothing that is oversized for you so that, if you must interact with others, you don't obviously appear healthy and well-fed. It's a strategy, sometimes part of the "gray man" approach, that is worth considering as times continue to get harder.

Alternatives and Supplements

Aside from transforming animal hides into clothing, something that's not as easy as you might assume, it is possible to fashion clothing from an assortment of materials if you can sew and don't much care how you look. Therefore, include an assortment of sewing supplies in your list of materials to purchase, particularly needles and plenty of thread. Assorted fabrics, buttons, and zippers may prove useful as well.

Again, quality shoes are far more important than most people realize, and, as you might suspect, are difficult to fashion on your own. That said, it is possible to create makeshift shoes—let's call them makeshift sandals—from wood, grass, animal hides, and tire treads with the right knowledge.[20,21,22,23]

Wide-brim hats, such as Boonie hats or cowboy hats, deserve a brief mention here because they do a fantastic job of keeping the sun off your face and neck, minimizing sunburns and heat stroke.

Remember to care for these crucial items better than you might otherwise. Sew rips and snags upon discovery and clean off and dry boots after heavy use, and they'll last you that much longer.

Glasses, Contacts, and Hearing Aids

Most people wear glasses or hearing aids only to help them in specific situations, such as only wearing glasses when reading a book or using hearing aids during conversation. But there are others who absolutely rely on these items to function day to day. Without them, these folks cannot operate, even at the most basic level in their daily lives. If you're one of them, imagine how difficult life will be if you break or lose your glasses or hearing aids, but there's little expectation of obtaining a replacement for months or years to come because they're too expensive to purchase or the materials simply aren't being made. That would be a real problem.

I realize many people keep a spare pair of glasses or contacts on hand just in case, but we're trying to prepare for the worst. With this in mind, I suggest that if your prescription doesn't change often, and certainly if you wear contacts daily, that you buy several pairs of eyeglasses. Fortunately, you can purchase prescription glasses online, often for a fraction of the cost you would pay at a brick and mortar store.[24] If your prescription changes more frequently, I encourage you to talk with your eye doctor to determine the best course of action. Ensure the doctor fully understands your desires to prepare for years down the road now, and not only until your prescription changes.

Hearing aids continue to be significantly more costly than glasses, even when purchased online. There are less expensive options available if you only take the time to look.[25] In addition, there are alternatives to traditional hearing aids, called sound amplification devices, some of which cost as little as thirty dollars as of this writing.[26] Of course, such devices don't offer near the quality or comfort of traditional hearing aids, but they may be just the thing if you've got nothing else to rely upon. And if your hearing aids use batteries, buy plenty of extras.

Alternatives and Supplements

When's the last time you've handled a magnifying glass? Although one might help in some situations, it won't fix real vision problems. Instead, consider laser eye surgery, such as LASIK. Although rarely covered by insurance, some companies provide discounts on LASIK, or may just help you save up for the procedure via a health savings account.[27] That said, be sure to discuss the pros and cons of such a procedure with your eye doctor and, for goodness' sake, go to a reputable provider.

Self-Defense and Safety

I know people who would put self-defense items, specifically firearms, at the top of any list like this one, and for good reason—the world is sometimes dangerous during the best of times. I can only imagine how much more dangerous things might become when the world all but implodes. But who's to really say how things will play out for you or where you live. After all, I've heard of stories where entire war zones are perfectly peaceful only a few blocks away from the actual fighting. But the problem is that bad things often occur out of nowhere. It's always better to have some ability to protect yourself and your loved ones than not.

Firearms, like them or not, are perhaps the only tool that the average person has at their disposal to even a life and death fight. Knives cannot make this claim. Tasers cannot make this claim. Martial arts cannot make this claim. Nothing else can either. Firearms are, as they say, the great equalizer.

What to purchase is up to you. What I can say is that you must (1) follow all federal, state, and local laws regarding your ability to own firearms, and (2) learn to use them safely and responsibly. Firearms use by people unfamiliar with them is just asking for trouble. Besides, you'll be far less able to defend yourself should the need ever arise if you don't practice with them regularly. There's a certain comfort level—and confidence—that comes with regular firearms practice, both of which will be welcome should you ever need to defend yourself. Find a qualified instructor if you're new to firearms. There are NRA firearms training courses all over the country, and many people are willing to help.

Regarding ammunition: The short answer is to buy as much as you reasonably can now because most of us can't predict what will be available down the road. Prices are still high for some calibers, which may affect your choice of firearms to purchase. Talk with a local gun store owner or firearms enthusiasts to get a better idea of the best firearms to purchase.

Body armor, as much as I shudder to suggest it, may be a wise investment in a post-collapse world. There are a wide variety of options available, including carrier styles, plates, protection levels, and more to consider—notably proper sizing—so it's nothing to take lightly.[28] Whatever you settle on, purchase from a reputable source, such as Spartan Armor or AR500.[29,30] Additional tactical gear may be of use, but I would focus on the essentials noted above, given their relative expense. Leave the tactical gear to those with the experience to use it properly.

Alternatives and Supplements

I get that some people either won't purchase firearms (because they fear them) or can't (because of where they live), so let's talk alternatives.

If firearms aren't an option, you could use several items to potentially disable an attacker, assuming you have the element of surprise on your side, among many other assumptions. Fairly obvious ideas, such as a knife, baseball bat, golf club, hammer, hefty wrench, large flashlight, or solid frying pan, would deal a serious blow to most people. A stun gun could be of use, too, but they have their problems. The biggest concern is that everything mentioned requires you to be within arm's length to use, which means you're within an attacker's reach, which isn't ideal.

Many companies make stand-off self-defense gear, such as pepper spray, pepper ball guns, and Tasers, but these devices could backfire in unexpected ways, like pepper spray drifting back in your face or, worse, the attacker is unaffected by it. Realize, too, that Tasers don't always penetrate clothing. Some say wasp spray would be devastating to spray in someone's face (and possibly illegal, too). I can imagine a wide variety of chemicals that would be less-than-pleasant to be sprayed with, but these could backfire on you as well. No matter what you might choose, you still have to subdue an attacker at some point, which makes these alternatives only temporary.

Disorientation devices could be momentarily useful, such as bright flashlights, strobe lights, lasers in the eye, flashbangs, and maybe a personal alarm, but I doubt it. Again, you still need to deal with the threat. What then?

I would also encourage you to focus on deterring or delaying an intruder. It's a fact that burglars don't like to be seen or identified. Lights, especially motion-activated outdoor lights, are useful to give criminals pause. Purchase battery-powered, motion-activated lights for times when the grid is down. Although not nearly as bright as their hard-wired counterparts, they're better than nothing. Dogs are often good at detecting intruders, though it depends on the breed.

Criminals prefer the most easily accessible entry point—doors and windows. Let's focus on doors to start.

Door security can be beefed-up in several ways, including installing long-throw deadbolts, upgrading strike plates, replacing door jamb molding, adding secondary latches/locks, and replacing door hinge screws with three-inch long wood screws. If money is tight—and even if it isn't—I would also suggest a door security bar, wedge, or barricade to prevent kick-ins. Address all exterior doors.

More drastic actions might include:

- Replacing any exterior door that isn't solid wood or metal with one that is.
- Replacing doors with large glass panes.
- Sliding glass patio doors should, at minimum, be replaced with solid French doors, but even these aren't very secure because of the way they latch. (Use a Katy bar or other security bar to reinforce French doors.)

It should go without saying, but keeping doors and windows locked is a good thing. There's no need to make things easier on the bad guys. Moreover, some criminals will go straight to the front door, ring the doorbell or knock, then wait for someone to answer before barging right in. Keep up your guard.

Windows are a bigger concern than doors because, as we all know, glass breaks. A large enough rock will shatter most windowpanes, and considering that most homes are full of windows, this is a real problem. One option is to use window security film, but it's not cheap, and a person will eventually make their way inside given enough time. Another idea is to board up windows with half-inch or thicker plywood, but it's not cheap either, and doing so will reduce escape routes. If this interests you, perhaps the best option is to strategically board up windows, such as the most easily accessible ground floor windows. It might even be useful to pre-cut and number sheets to each window so they can be more quickly installed should the need arise.

Now's a good time to briefly mention your ability to evacuate on matter the reason. Several useful actions include:

- Have more than one escape route identified for each room should fire block the main exit.
- Don't use keyed locks on the insides of doors because keys may be misplaced.
- Keep a flashlight at each bedside in case the power goes out at night.
- Have easy to put on shoes next to the bed to avoid cutting your feet from broken glass or other hazards.
- Purchase a fire escape ladder for second-story egress, if necessary.
- Determine where household members will regroup outside the home.

Whatever actions you take, always consider your ability to evacuate, such as during a house fire or other natural disaster, so don't go crazy boarding up all of your doors and windows for fear an intruder. Take your time enacting changes that make sense for your situation and which don't put you or your family in unnecessary danger.

Part 2: Items to Aid Your Survival Until Society Stabilizes

If the items listed in part one are a bridge for when the unprepared masses wake up, consider the items discussed in part two as your lifeline. They're meant to keep you several steps ahead of the many folks who will become desperate because they do not know how to survive when the grid goes down, the water stops flowing, and the grocery stores no longer have food.

I don't entirely blame them. After all, it's easy to become complacent, particularly when our modern society makes life so easy. But these same people will be the same ones begging—even demanding—that the government (or you) give them something, anything, when they have nothing. You don't want to be one of them.

Part two will differ from part one, in that, while I will continue to recommend a wide variety of items to purchase, items I own myself, I will also offer advice and thoughts on how to survive when times get really hard. For instance, there's only so much you can purchase to keep cool without a functioning air conditioner, but there's a lot you can do to help the situation, like shading the morning sun and ensuring a cross-breeze. Similarly, I can't properly discuss refrigeration alternatives, such as a root cellar, because it's not exactly something that can be purchased outright. I hope that makes sense. Let's get started.

Have you ever had to live without grid power for more than, say, a day? I don't mean when you've planned on it, such as during a camping or hiking trip for the weekend, but while you're still at home? If not, you may be shocked at how crucial the electrical grid is to your everyday life.

Sure, we all know that the lights and refrigerator won't work when the power goes out, but they're only the beginning of your troubles if a power outage lasts for weeks or merely becomes inconsistent, unreliable, or cost prohibitive.

For starters, the air conditioner certainly won't operate without grid power. Similarly, you may be unable to heat your home if you don't have a supplemental heat source, such as a woodstove. Both situations will be uncomfortable, if not deadly.

It may surprise you to hear that your municipal water supply needs power to operate; even gravity fed water towers will eventually require power to resupply their tanks. Most well water pumps need power, too.

Municipal sewer systems—as well as some septic systems—need power to function. Without power, you could eventually find that sewage has backed up through your drains, which wouldn't be pleasant on so many levels, including being hazardous to your health.

Most cooktop stoves—and nearly every oven—need grid power to function. Without it, cooking a meal may become a real chore, especially if you're forced to cook outside over a campfire in the dead of winter.

Even the vast majority of our entertainment is based on the grid functioning, from watching television or online videos to playing video games and connecting with friends. An extended loss of grid power may truly send a generation or two into deep despair.

And those are only the typical problems we'll all face. Some of us know full-well that home-based medical equipment needs power to operate, a lack of which can logically become deadly quickly. Power tools need electricity to be of any use—even battery-operated ones will need recharged fairly soon—which means you may be unable to repair damage to your home in a timely manner.

Not having reliable or affordable power is a serious problem. And if I'm being honest, I don't have a great "one size fits all" solution. There are options, though none of them are ideal, and some aren't cheap. But you will want to make choices now or possibly suffer the consequences later. At the very least, you'll need to learn to do more while relying less on the grid.

And these are only the concerns with a partial loss of grid power, all-encompassing as it is in our lives. What about a loss of the fire department or police? Civil unrest is a real possibility. Martial law may quickly become welcomed by law-abiding citizens. Could you defend yourself and your loved ones until then? How about extinguishing a fire that spreads from your neighbor's house? I expect small fires to be the norm, particularly as people do a variety of things they shouldn't. How about a loss of our healthcare system? How devastating that would be to the tens of millions of people who rely on it day in and day out to treat both chronic and acute conditions.

I could also explain how we'll likely see major infrastructure problems as roadways and bridges become increasingly neglected. Or, I could point out that insects and even wildlife will encroach into our lives and homes with each passing day. You probably also know that caring for pets may become difficult if pet food or veterinarian services become scarce or prohibitively expensive. I could go on, but these are relatively minor concerns compared to the bigger issues mentioned at the start.

We simply can't fix all our troubles merely by purchasing everything now. This is primarily because some of what we'll invariably need requires specific knowledge, such as healthcare and veterinarian services, or specialized equipment, such as heavy machinery to build or maintain roadways.

But we can still do a lot for ourselves, especially if we focus on procuring the right equipment and supplies to help us survive until society truly stabilizes. To do so, we'll tackle the aforementioned concerns in the order brought up. We'll focus on a lack of lighting, refrigeration, air conditioning, and heating to start, then move on to a lack of water, sewers, stoves, and so on.

Remember, part two will focus on those items—and actions—you can take to be more self-sufficient. It's entirely possible that these solutions may not work for you or your situation, and they may cause you to spend money on items that you may never use, so consider these purchases carefully.

Also, I expect you'll have some land to use, even if it's only a small yard. You don't need a lot, but you need something to work with, such as when cooking food outdoors, collecting rainwater, and burying trash. Consider how each suggestion fits with your living situation and adjust as necessary. Now, let's talk about solutions to these very specific problems.

Lighting

Not being able to see in the dark, particularly when we're so accustomed to doing so, can be problematic for adults and downright scary for young children. Luckily, this is a relatively easy problem to fix in the short term by purchasing lanterns and flashlights. For daily, around the house use, battery-powered LED lanterns are great because they're very efficient, safe for children and pets, and should last as long or longer than their fuel-powered counterparts.[31]

LED flashlights, like lanterns, are relatively efficient and inexpensive, too.[32] I prefer smaller, handheld options for around the house, and larger, often brighter, flashlights for outdoor use.[33,34]

Realize that there are many lantern and flashlight options available. They come in all shapes and sizes and use a variety of battery styles (e.g., AA, AAA, D-cell). Some are rechargeable, but often use an irreplaceable battery, which I don't recommend. If possible, try to purchase lanterns and flashlights that use AA or AAA batteries only—rather than D-cell or unusual battery sizes—so that you can use the batteries in a variety of equipment. Buy a handful of lanterns and several flashlights at minimum, so that (1) you can stash them in strategic places around the house, (2) everyone will have one, and (3) you have backups in case one or more breaks.

Battery Choices

Perhaps the only problem you'll have is stockpiling enough batteries to run them for many months or years on end. You can remedy this to an extent by purchasing one- or two-hundred alkaline batteries, which are relatively inexpensive right now and will remain viable for many years. The Amazon Basics brand of batteries is a good choice for the price.[35] Just ensure you purchase the correct batteries, usually either AA or AAA, for the equipment you purchase. In fact, opting for equipment that uses the same size batteries are preferable, though not always attainable.

Including rechargeable batteries—Eneloop is a quality brand—will ensure you have battery power for years to come.[36] Be sure to add in an appropriate battery charger, otherwise they will become useless rather quickly.[37] Whether you intend to rely on grid power to recharge your rechargeable batteries is up to you, but so long as the grid doesn't completely fail, that choice should be fine considering how little power these batteries take to recharge. If you'd like added insurance, you can purchase a solar-powered battery charger or an alkaline battery charger, though my experience with these and similar items has been wanting.[38,39] It's a much better idea to create a small off-grid power setup, which we'll discuss later.

Why You Should Avoid Candles

I know people who swear by stockpiling candles for long-term power outages, but they're an unnecessary fire hazard for such purposes. While it's one thing to light a few candles around the bathtub for an hour, it's quite another to rely on them for hours on end, likely all around the house, and as your primary source of lighting. Add in pets or young children who might inadvertently knock them over, that candles produce little light, and the likelihood that over time you won't use them as safely as you should, makes candles not worth the risk. If you see things differently, then consider a candle holder, such as this hurricane-style candle holder, or something similar to be as safe as possible.[40]

Alternatives and Supplements

Other battery-powered options include patio solar lights and wall tap lights. Patio lights are useful because they can be set outside during the day to charge, then brought inside at night. They'll typically last all night long and should provide enough light to keep from tripping over things. Similarly, tap lights are LED-style lights that usually use replaceable batteries, can be secure to walls with double-sided tape, and typically provide enough light to keep from stubbing a toe.

You may be tempted to purchase a hand-crank light, but my experience has been less than ideal. They're a lot of work to get any real runtime out of them, and most are cheaply constructed. Avoid hand-crank lights.

While I'm a huge fan of battery-operated lighting because they're inexpensive, safe, and long-lasting, assuming you don't purchase the cheapest option available, they're not the only alternative. In fact, many people continue to prefer their gas-powered counterparts—kerosene, propane, or Coleman white gas—when camping and during blackouts.

A big reason they're still popular is because gas lanterns, such as the Coleman Duel Fuel Lantern, are often much brighter than battery-powered options, so if you're intending to light up a large area outdoors, then gas lanterns are the better choice.[41] Gas lanterns can last years, even decades, if properly cared for, and they're usually safe so long as you're paying attention to what you're doing.

But they can be a burn hazard, occasionally require maintenance, such as needing to replace the mantle or globe if it breaks, and must have fuel to operate, which could become a storage hazard in large quantities or even be unavailable. And, of course, you would never want to use any gas lantern indoors because of carbon monoxide buildup.

54

All that said, there's no harm in having options. If you can find a great deal on a gas-powered lantern or two, such as at a clearance sale or, better yet, at a garage sale, then grab it. Just be sure to purchase extra mantles or wicks and fuel.

Whatever lighting options you choose, be sure you understand how to maintain them, and definitely how to use them safely. After all, the last problem you should have to deal with during hard times is one of your own doing.

Refrigeration

Your refrigerator not working is potentially a bigger problem than not having lighting, but it's not insurmountable. You can start by consolidating. We, for example, have three large refrigerators, a huge chest freezer, and two mini fridges in our house. Yes, that's a lot, but all the women who live with me—my wife, my mother-in-law, and my mother—insist. (You can feel sorry for me later. For now, keep reading.) When hard times come, this situation will no longer be tenable. We'll be forced to consolidate down to our most efficient refrigerator at most.

Interestingly, a modern chest freezer can be considerably more efficient than a refrigerator, though how efficient depends on a variety of factors, such as usage habits, ambient temperature, respective efficiency ratings, the relative size of each appliance, and more. While I've never tried it, some people have converted a chest freezer into a super efficient refrigerator, which may be worth the effort if you don't mind DIY projects like this.[42]

Alternatively, they do manufacture fairly efficient and relatively inexpensive mini fridges these days. It might, therefore, be wise to purchase one and only use it to store those foods most susceptible to spoilage, such as meat and dairy. Search local classified ads to avoid paying full price or shop sales.

It would also be wise to understand which foods don't actually need refrigeration, such as many fruits, vegetables, and condiments, to conserve precious refrigerator space.[43]

Alternatives and Supplements

One project we'll be working on soon is a walk-in root cellar, which is essentially a large hole in the ground where you can store root vegetables, like carrots and potatoes, for months without refrigeration. Even some fruits, such as apples and pears, and nuts, can be stored for months without concern.

But you don't need to rent an excavator to build one as fancy as we intend to. I've seen people bury a refrigerator or even a trash can to act as a makeshift root cellar.[44] Anything that can be buried in the ground while simultaneously protecting food from water and insects should work for short-term usage. Realize, too, that you'll need to allow for proper airflow into the makeshift root cellar so the vegetables don't get moldy and rot. Albeit old, a good book on the topic is *Root Cellaring: Natural Cold Storage of Fruits & Vegetables* by Mike Bubel.[45]

Let me be clear: A root cellar is no substitute for refrigeration. The most susceptible foods, specifically meat and dairy, must be kept at forty degrees Fahrenheit or less to prevent bacteria along with other undesirable organisms from growing.

While it's possible that a properly constructed root cellar can reach temperatures down into the forties Fahrenheit, they all fluctuate several degrees or more throughout the year no matter what.

A root cellar's temperature will depend on your latitude, where it's constructed on your land, what materials you make the root cellar from, and so much more. No doubt there's a lot to consider before building one if you want the best performance possible.

Regardless, almost any root cellar will suffice for a majority of foods that rarely require refrigeration to begin with. For those foods that need refrigeration, consider home canning, which we'll discuss next.

Canning Equipment

Maybe you're concerned that you won't have any power at all, not even for a mini fridge. Perhaps you've started a backyard garden and now you have tomatoes, zucchini, potatoes, and squash coming out of your ears... at least we usually do. Or maybe you've visited the local farmers' market and bought everything in sight. While you can certainly attempt to eat everything before it spoils, most people wouldn't dare. Instead, they do the neighborly thing and try to give their vegetables away to anyone who will take them. But if we assume hard times are coming, you're likely better off preserving these healthy vegetables instead. One great way to preserve them for a year or two is to can them in mason jars.

There are two primary methods of canning—water bath canning and pressure canning—the latter of which shouldn't be confused with a pressure cooker. The general rule of thumb is that low-acid foods, like animal products, must be pressure canned; highly acidic foods, such as fruits, pickled vegetables, sugar preserves, and tomatoes, can be safely processed in a boiling water bath canner.

To make certain you process your vegetables safely, purchase a book on canning. The *Ball Complete Book of Home Preserving* by Judi Kingry is a popular choice, although there are other options.[46] The important part is to follow a tried-and-true recipe. Doing so will ensure that you eliminate all harmful bacteria, which will help to keep you from getting sick.

I should mention that canning—even water bath canning—isn't a panacea, largely because it's a lot more work than most beginners realize. For starters, you must ensure a sterile environment, follow recipes closely, and even when you do everything correct, sometimes mason jars don't seal properly. But many people are excellent at canning. My in-laws, for instance, enjoy canning a variety of their garden haul, specifically by making salsa, jams, and more. Now, if I could just get them to label their canned foods properly, it would work out even better.

Most people, it seems, start with water bath canning because water bath canning doesn't require a lot of equipment. About all you really need is a large stockpot, a rack to keep the jars off the bottom of the pot, and some mason jars. I suggest purchasing a water bath canning set so you have everything you need to get started, besides the jars, lids, and bands, that is.[47]

And if you find you enjoy canning, unlike me, move on to pressure canning. Realize, however, that a quality pressure canner will cost you a few hundred dollars, which is a significant investment, but an investment not to take lightly because lesser pressure canners have exploded.[48]

What and How Much to Purchase

Aside from the initial investment in canning equipment, you'll need to purchase mason jars, lids, and bands. I prefer wide-mouth jars over regular mouth jars, but not everyone feels the same. I suggest you purchase a variety of jar sizes, mainly focusing on quart-sized, pint, and half-pint jars, as they are the most called for sizes in canning recipes. To avoid wasting money, buy a canning book before buying jars so that you might decide which foods it is that you most expect to can, and then you can determine which jars sizes to buy based on those expectations.

Realize, however, that while you can reuse glass mason jars, the glass weakens over time and may eventually crack after repeated use. It's usually not a tremendous concern, but purchase more jars than you feel you'll use initially as eventual replacements. Besides, it never hurts to have additional mason jars since they can be useful for storing more than just food.

How many jars should you purchase? Tough question. My advice is to start with a few dozen of your preferred sizes, try canning a few times, and then adjust your stockpile of jars as needed.

Realize, too, that you'll want to buy more bands than jars because, although bands can be reused like jars, they do rust over time, especially if you fail to remove and dry the bands after canning. Lids, unfortunately, cannot be reused even if they still look good because the wax melts and may not seal properly the next time. Buy many more lids if you expect to home can regularly. That said, Harvest Guard and Tattler make reusable canning lids, which I've never tried, though many people swear by them.[49]

Alternatives and Supplements

There are two main alternatives to canning, both of which have their advantages and disadvantages. The first, and likely easiest option, is dehydrating. I used to enjoy dehydrating vegetables using my Excalibur dehydrator.[50] These days, all I ever use it for is to make homemade yogurt. Why did I quit? Because the food never quite seemed to return to normal when we went to use it months or years later. Well, that and I absolutely stored the dehydrated food for years too long, which, as with home-canned foods, isn't recommended because it will eventually spoil.

I'm not saying the vegetables I dehydrated weren't edible or useable in soups within a year, they were, but the results weren't ideal. Besides, unless you purchase frozen vegetables—which are already blanched—from the grocery store, you'll need to blanch them before dehydrating can begin. In my case, dehydrating became too much of a hassle for what I received in return. That said, dehydrating is still a viable short-term storage option if you're only trying to preserve garden vegetables for the coming winter. If interested, I highly recommend the website, Dehydrate2Store.com where you'll find a wealth of knowledge about dehydrating, including tips, recipes, and more.[51]

Freeze-drying is another alternative to canning, and it's the best long-term food storage method available. Freeze-drying is so good, in fact, that I recently purchased a large Harvest Right freeze-dryer, which is no small investment.[52] There are many reasons freeze-drying is superior to all other options, but the biggest reasons center on the quality of the end product. In short, freeze-dried foods are more nutritious, almost always have better taste and texture, often reconstitute faster than their dehydrated counterparts, and can be stored for years—if not decades—without a loss in nutritional value or concern for your safety.

Whereas I used to purchase freeze-dried foods online and locally whenever I could, doing so is rather expensive, which is why I've opted to freeze-dry my produce in the future. I'm not suggesting you invest thousands of dollars in a freeze dryer of your own, and certainly not until you already have plenty of groceries stockpiled, a garden or orchard producing excess vegetables and fruits, and have also given canning a shot.

If you want to dehydrate or freeze-dry, then you're going to need either mason jars or Mylar bags depending on which option you choose. Mason jars are multipurpose, in that they must be used for storing wet food and can be used for storing dry foods, whereas Mylar bags are only useful for storing dry foods which have been dehydrated or freeze-dried. Personally, I use both jars and bags. I will also say that if you're going to use mason jars, then a vacuum sealer with a mason jar lid attachment is helpful.[53,54] No matter whether you opt for jars or Mylar bags, you'll need oxygen absorbers when storing any dry food. In addition, Mylar bags will require either an impulse sealer or a vacuum sealer. (Note: Reference this chart to size your oxygen absorbers correctly.[55])

Put another way, water bath canning and pressure canning require mason jars; dehydrating and freeze-drying will use mason jars or Mylar bags, both of which need oxygen absorbers; Mylar bags further require either an impulse sealer or a vacuum sealer.

I suggest you invest in home canning to start with if you've never attempted to process food on your own. There are decades of best practices to follow, and an entire industry ready to help you store food properly.

Air Conditioning

Not having a functional air conditioner is a problem, and not only because you may be utterly uncomfortable for months on end. Food, in particular, will spoil much faster in high temperatures—even traditional survival food, like meals-ready-to-eat (MREs), won't last long. In addition, relative humidity levels may become unacceptably high indoors, thus causing mold problems, and also affecting food storage. In fact, a lack of air conditioning will affect almost everything inside your home.

Running ceiling fans or box fans continuously will help circulate stagnant air. Attic fans and swamp coolers are options as well, though how well they'll work depends on your climate. At the very least, fans—in any form—are typically far less expensive to run than a central air conditioner and will help to a degree.

You can also take passive actions to ease the aforementioned problems to an extent, such as by opening windows to allow for a cross-breeze, shading the east and west sides of your home from the sun with tarps (which is one reason awnings were so popular before central air), and moving everything crucial—including you and your food—to the coolest area of your home.

As an example, where we live in the Midwest, basements are common. During the heat of the summer, the basement stays several degrees cooler than the rest of the house because hot air rises. There is also some benefit to a portion of our basement being earth-banked, which further facilitates some rooms in the basement staying cooler than others. My guess is the same must be true for your situation, even if to a lesser degree.

At minimum, I suggest having a few plug-in fans on hand. We prefer the inexpensive box fans. Place them in upper-story windows, facing outward, to remove hot air from the house. Better yet, this online article suggests you act strategically with your fan usage, stating, "To establish cross breezes, don't think in just two dimensions. A fan in the door will move air, and another in the window will do the same—but if you set them up strategically, the door fan can blow cool air onto you while the window fan pulls hot air away."[56]

I would also purchase additional window screen material, along with spline and a roller tool, if you expect to keep your windows open regularly.

What About Using a Window Air Conditioner Instead?

It's true that you don't *need* to cool your entire home. You could, for example, choose to only cool a single room using a window air conditioner, but there's a catch. Although most window units use from several hundred up to a thousand watts of power or more—far less than a central air conditioning unit, which uses, on average, a few thousand watts of power while running—central units tend not to run continuously, whereas window units often do.

In fact, you could run a window unit far longer—even continuously—in order to cool a single room, all while thinking it's using substantially less power only to find out you're not. As an example, let's say your central unit uses three thousand watts of power, a low-end average, and runs for eight hours over the course of a day during the summer months. Total power usage would equal 24,000 watts, or 24 kWh. Running a one-thousand watt window air conditioner for the same eight hours would only use 8,000 watts, or 8 kWh.

That sounds like huge savings, and it is on the face, but odds are that you'll need to run a window unit much longer to achieve the same amount of cooling as the central unit can achieve in less time. There are many reasons for this, including window units being less efficient, the rest of the house is now warmer than usual because the central unit isn't running, higher humidity levels in the home (also because the central unit isn't running) which holds heat, more people and pets occupying a much smaller space, and so on.

Of course, how long a central air conditioning system will run fluctuates because of a variety of factors, such as your climate, the time of year, your home's insulation, whether your central air conditioner is in good working condition, and more.

It may be best to block off entire sections of your home, such as the entire upstairs or rooms you never use, yet still allow the central air conditioner to run. Yes, this will eventually cause problems for the portion of the house not receiving air conditioning, but it should reduce overall power usage to an extent if you're desperate.

Another option is to only run the central unit's fan, which usually consumes less than a thousand watts of power, without also running the air-conditioner. By so doing, you're still circulating air, providing a slight cooling effect, and also helping to reduce humidity levels, yet consuming far less power. This option probably won't work well for those who live in very humid climates.

Ultimately, the answer whether paying to run a whole-house unit is better than a single window unit or the central unit fan alone isn't straightforward. What I can say is that this lengthy discussion assumes you still have regular, albeit expensive, power. But what if you don't have any power at all?

Alternatives and Supplements

Staying hydrated is a good starting point since the human body must sweat to stay cool. You could also take cold showers or even wrap a cool washrag around your neck and wrists for temporary relief. Wearing breathable clothing is also a good idea. I would definitely close blinds or curtains to shade the sun, and open other windows to generate a cross-breeze. Don't run appliances indoors during the heat of the day. Buy a dehumidifier. Sit outdoors in the shade. But you probably know all of this already. What else can you really do? Following are a few more thoughts that most people don't consider.

You'd be surprised at how much radiant heat enters your home via sunlight, both through windows and the rest of your home's building envelope. Consider using blackout curtains or dark window tint on the most troublesome windows, though some folks use aluminum foil, shiny side out, instead. Install a radiant barrier in the attic or improve the attic's insulation.[57] Feeling really desperate? Paint your roof shingles white. Alright, that's over the top. In fact, this online article states that doing so is not enough to make a sizeable difference: "When comparing a totally white shingle to a totally black shingle, the attic temperature may increase 8-10 degrees. However, when you get into the grays, browns and tans, there is only a 2-3 degree difference. Also, an 8 degree increase in attic temperature does not mean an 8 degree increase in your house."[58] So much for me painting my roof shingles white this weekend.

Most passive cooling ideas need to be incorporated into the home's design right from the start. For instance, the number of windows and even window orientation, as seemingly inconsequential as that may appear, makes a considerable difference in heat retention in the summer and heat loss in the winter.[59] A preference for high ceilings, the general orientation of your house relative to the sun's trajectory, and planting shade trees on the east and west sides of your house can make a big difference, too. But few homeowners, and even fewer builders, ever consider such things.

We're stuck with homes, apartments, and condominiums that all but require central air-conditioning, which means you'll need to work with your home's design rather than against it.

Heating

Keeping yourself warm is easier than staying cool, though both extreme heat and extreme cold can be killers. You can certainly layer clothing as desired, huddle together, and wrap yourself in warm blankets to keep your teeth from chattering, to name a few obvious ideas.

I won't rehash clothing here except to say that you should have clothing which will keep you warm without heat, whether indoors or out. In fact, I would have different warm clothing for indoors and outdoors; doing so will reduce laundry consumption.

In addition, sleeping bags are a tried-and-true option; every family member should have one. There's no reason to buy anything fancy, but you want it to have a good amount of insulation, which means you should look at a three-season bag or, if you live in the frigid north, a cold-weather sleeping bag. But if you can get a good deal on anything, such as at a garage sale, grab whatever you can.

But you probably won't want to hop around in a sleeping bag or dress like an Eskimo all day long either, so aside from these passive ideas, it's wise to have a supplemental source of heat, like a wood-burning stove. You'll want to ensure the stove has been properly inspected and cleaned recently—at least yearly—and that you have plenty of seasoned firewood (you may need a few cords for a single winter), as well as the ability to make kindling, and matches or lighters to start the fire with. Fire starters are very useful here, too.[60] I would include a handful of boxes for other uses, such as when starting a campfire for cooking purposes or heating water.

Propane and kerosene space heaters are another short-term option, though they'll require you to stockpile plenty of fuel. If given the option between propane and kerosene, choose a kerosene heater for cost, ease of use, and fuel storage considerations.[61] As with anything that burns fuel, ensure the heater is safe for indoor use, has extra wicks (and batteries if it uses an electric starter), and store the kerosene fuel in an approved container.

Alternatives and Supplements

There are interesting ways to keep warm, including makeshift stoves, such as the rocket mass heater touted by Paul Wheaton, among others.[62] If you're building a home or off-grid cabin, or you don't mind a big remodel, then ideas such as this are wonderful to incorporate as they will use far less firewood and are possibly safer than the traditional wood-burning stove we all know and love.

You could incorporate passive solar heating of some sort, or purchase an electric blanket or heating pad—

connected to an off-grid solar setup, discussed later—
to keep your core warm while you sleep.[63]

Other passive solutions include insulating windows
with plain bubble wrap, using reflective foil insulation
to reflect and insulate a small room, and stockpiling
hand warmers.[64]

Once you understand that the trick to keeping warm
is to reduce the transfer of heat from a warmer
environment (like your body or home) to a colder one
(like the outside) then you can take actions to
mitigate it. I should caution you, though, that you'll
want some exchange of air between the outside
world and warm inside or else you may suffer oxygen
deprivation due to carbon dioxide buildup, so don't
go overboard. Airflow is a good thing.

Always start with keeping yourself warm, then focus
on the room, then your home, if possible.

Water

The average family uses over three-hundred gallons of water per day. According to research conducted by the Water Research Foundation, 24% is used solely for flushing toilets, 20% is for showering or bathing, 19% comes straight out of the faucet—most likely for personal hygiene uses or washing dishes—17% is for washing clothes, and 20% is a catch-all, including water leaks.[65,66]

I'd say we're wasting a lot of good, clean water when we don't have to. What happens to your daily routine if the water stops flowing or becomes unusable, such as after a flood, algae bloom, or other contamination event, like radium, lead, or man-made chemicals?[67] Probably not much if the event is only temporary, but I suspect your habits (and priorities) around water usage will change drastically should anything like that ever happen, and certainly if you're forced to collect your own water.

For starters, you certainly won't be wasting water on frivolous uses, like washing your car or watering the lawn. You'll probably only flush the toilet when necessary. We may wear clothing for longer periods of time in order to avoid washing them. Even a sponge bath may become a weekly activity. Many drastic actions may become necessary.

What I know is that most households cannot continue to use three-hundred gallons of water each day if they had to collect it on their own. I also know that because water is such a crucial resource, we cannot ignore a lack of water.

Water Storage Options

Fortunately, getting your water usage down to the bare minimum of, say, five or ten gallons per person per day is possible. But we need to have some water stored to begin with, and it needs to be kept in something durable. There are few containers better than a typical rain barrel. Personally, we use 55-gallon, FDA-approved water barrels, like these.

But even a plastic trash can is better than nothing. Realize, however, that we do not consider most plastics safe because they will, over time, leech unwanted chemicals into the water. If you're storing water temporarily, and you have no other choice, then I wouldn't concern myself with leeching chemicals, but it's not an ideal solution. Even if you don't intend to store water for long-term, potable water containers, like the rain barrels shown above, are always best.

Another option is 270- or 330-gallon IBC totes. They're great for rooftop rainwater collection, and store five or six times as much as a typical rain barrel. Here's a setup, which is still a work in progress. I started it this summer for watering our garden.

The good news is that you can often find rainwater barrels and IBC totes on Facebook Marketplace or Craigslist at fair prices. Just do your best to ensure that any used water storage container you purchase second-hand contained nothing unfit for human consumption, such as solvents, lubricants, or other industrial chemicals. The seller, assuming they're being honest, will know what they previously contained. Also, even a thorough cleaning will not make the water fit for human consumption because chemical residues can remain indefinitely, some of which will make you very ill. But if you're concerned about sourcing these containers used, you can always purchase them new, albeit at a significant price hike.

There are other, even larger options, along with ways to store water using the layout of the land, but rain barrels and IBC totes are usually the easiest way for the average homeowner to get started.

Water Usage Habits

Understand that even storing several hundred gallons of water in a dozen rain barrels won't last long if your water-usage habits don't also change drastically. Even if we assume you can get your water usage down to ten gallons per person, a single 55-gallon rain barrel will barely last five days, whereas a 330-gallon IBC tote will last a month. That's a vast difference, and one more reason IBC totes are so useful.

Regardless of the water containers you choose, your habits must change if we're to ensure you'll have water for weeks or months. My best suggestions follow:

- Flush toilets only when necessary. Follow the motto, "if it's yellow, let it mellow" at the very least. If things get more drastic, use a bucket and lid to hold waste products, then dump or bury the bucket contents outside, away from food and water sources.
- Limit all bathing to an *as needed* basis, and definitely curtail bathing time. For example, turn the shower on to wet yourself down, turn off as you soap up, then briefly turn on again to rinse off. If things get worse, rarely shower. Instead, wet a washcloth and use that to wipe yourself down, focusing on your face, armpits, groin, hands, and feet. Also, store bath water for flushing toilets.
- Never let the faucet run while brushing your teeth, shaving, doing dishes, or any reason.
- Learn to use the three-bin method to wash dishes.[68] You'll need to stockpile bleach for this to be truly effective, and may need multiple plastic containers or commercial bus tubs to perform this method properly.[69] You may want to save this water for flushing toilets.

- Be capable of washing laundry by hand. I'll admit, doing laundry by hand isn't easy, and it will reduce the longevity of most clothing we wear. Washing by hand may also require special equipment, such as a washboard or Wonderwash, clothesline or rack, clothespins, and special laundry bar soap, like Fels-Naptha, to name the more obvious needs.[70,71]
- Remember water for your pets, too. Treat their water and foods needs as you would any other person.

Water Treatment Options

Having stored water is only a part of the solution. Any water you collect, no matter whether it's from a nearby stream or your rooftop, must be seen as unfit for human consumption, because it probably is. After all, water may be contaminated with bacteria from animal droppings, toxic metals, dust, pollen, mold, and other concerns. Even pure rainwater can pick up airborne contaminants. Therefore, all water that you collect needs to be treated before consumption, even if never directly consumed, such as when brushing your teeth.

They often tout boiling water as the best method available to most of us. It's great for killing off pathogens, like bacteria, but not so good at removing toxic metals or other airborne contaminants. Boiling water is also resource intensive, so relying on it over a long period is unrealistic. Bleach, too, has its problems, and isn't a long-term solution either.

This is where filters come in handy. I'm a big fan of the Berkey water filter systems because their Black Berkey filters are great at filtering out much of the nasty stuff I expect to encounter when collecting rainwater.[72] We've used ours for many years without trouble, but then again, we're not using it to filter rainwater daily, so I can't say that it's a perfect solution. I keep our Berkey system around—along with extra filters—just in case we ever need it. I should point out that there are knock-off filters available, some of which I've tried, and none of which I would bet my life on. Stick with the name brand Berkey filters to be certain they'll work.

If you prefer a less expensive option, the Sawyer Mini is a great alternative.[73] Purchase a few of these filters, convert one or more into a gravity filter if you like, know how to properly backwash it, and you'll have a reliable water filter for years to come.[74,75]

There are plenty of other choices available if you prefer something else, including alternative gravity filter systems. You can even make your own gravity filter for a fraction of the cost using their Black Berkey filters, two five-gallon buckets, and a spigot.[76] I've done it, and it's fairly easy.

Whatever option you choose, stay away from any filter for at-home use that cannot filter a few thousand gallons of water over its lifetime, which leaves out most backpacking filters. I suspect you will probably filter hundreds of gallons of water each month for a single person alone. Multiply that by a household and you could easily filter more than a thousand gallons in a single month.

I should also mention that for the best results, combine treatment options. First filter water through a quality gravity water filter, then boil it (preferred) or treat it chemically, such as with bleach. Doing so will better ensure that any water you collect is as safe as possible for human consumption.

I realize that boiling water will not be easy long-term, which is why we'll discuss a handy way to pasteurize water shortly using the sun. If you set things up properly and stick with it, you'll have a constant source of trustworthy water for drinking, cooking, and other basic personal hygiene needs.

Bleach, among other chemicals, like iodine, are potential alternatives to boiling (or pasteurizing) water. That said, I wouldn't want to rely on bleach specifically over the long-term because there are better uses for it, I'd need to stockpile a lot when I don't have to, and it's not healthy for human use over months or years. It is a very temporary solution only. I can say the same for iodine treatments.

Alternatives and Supplements

Tarps, which we'll get to shortly, may prove quite useful for collecting clean rainwater, at least as much as hoped for, because you can string them up and funnel what they collect directly into a rain barrel, bucket, or bin, completely bypassing your rooftop and all their potential contaminants. Buy a few 6'x8' or 10'x12' heavy-duty tarps and label them only for collecting rainwater. Remember to put them up when not used for rainwater collection to avoid unnecessary contamination. Finally, consider where and how you'll string up these tarps.[77] Maybe even try it.

Buckets, which we'll also get to shortly, along with funnels, are useful for transferring water from larger containers to smaller ones, something you may do regularly. You'll also need a water barrel pump or siphon hose if you opt for rain barrels.[78,79] Window screen material, which I briefly mentioned elsewhere, may come in handy here as well for keeping bugs and debris out of barrel bung openings.

Water, like food, is crucial to life. Its importance cannot be ignored, and I promise you will kick yourself if you neglect your water needs while you can still do something about it.

Waste Disposal

What's that old saying about owing more of your health to a plumber than your doctor? I don't know how truthful that is these days, especially as we age, but I can say that without functional plumbing— coupled with a clean source of water—expect more diseases to crop up, some of which can be a very serious problem. Keeping yourself healthy, therefore, is one major reason water usage must be reserved for the most crucial of uses. Your health is also why stockpiling a wide assortment of cleaners, particularly hand soap, is such a good idea.

Back to sewers. Have you ever thought about what happens if your sewer system stops functioning for an extended period, say, weeks or months? Although there are many factors involved, it's entirely possible that raw sewage could back up into your drains and flood portions of your home. A mess doesn't even describe what kind of problem that could become. The bad part is that you probably have drains all over your house. Most of us have three or more drains in each bathroom—one each for the shower or tub, sink, and toilet. There are also drains in the kitchen, laundry room, perhaps one solely for your central HVAC, and probably one or more in the basement if you have one.

Now, if you live on an upper level of a condo or apartment, this might not be such a concern initially. But you may quickly find that flushing anything down your drains won't work because the lower apartment drains are also clogged.

How to Prevent Backflow

I have seen people suggest stuffing racquetball balls down drains or in mainlines, but I don't recommend it. Instead, consider a flood guard or backwater valve.[80] This video demonstrates how they work, but the idea is that a float rises to create a seal if the drain pipes flow backwards.[81] Unfortunately, you'll need one for each drain, so they're not useful everywhere. Perhaps a basement or lower floor drain is the best spot because it's most likely to flood first. I believe they also make backflow prevention devices for mainlines, but I'd have to imagine that would be expensive to install if you don't already have one. Either way, talk with a qualified plumber about options if this solution interests you.

How are Septic Systems Affected?

The good news is that most septic systems shouldn't have a problem with backflow problems unless they require electricity to operate and you continue trying to use your septic with no power. But so long as your system is gravity-fed, you're treating the system properly by not flushing items that don't belong (e.g., facial tissue, grease, oils), and you have it pumped every few years, then you should be fine for years.

Proper Waste Disposal

Find a good place in your yard to dump waste products. Ideally, this should be well away from any water or food source, away from the house, and hopefully nowhere that pets or animals will get into it. How far is that? Most people will say a few hundred feet, which could end up being a corner of the backyard or even further away. The reason this is so crucial is that the bad microorganisms in fecal matter can migrate over time and contaminate resources, such as your vegetable garden and groundwater, without you realizing it. Urine is less of a concern than fecal matter, but there's no harm in being cautious because urine also contains some potentially harmful microorganisms.

Fecal matter, in particular, should be buried a few feet deep if possible—or layered if you have no choice—and disposed of separately from urine. In fact, if you intend to use buckets to contain waste products in your home prior to disposal outdoors, then use one bucket for urine and one for fecal matter. Doing so will help keep the smell down, reduces the amount of fecal matter to dispose of, and is safer to dispose of separately over the long-term for several reasons.

Believe it or not, some people even compost their fecal waste for their garden, but you really need to do your research before attempting to treat human waste (known as humanure) like cow manure.[82]

Layering the fecal matter bucket between uses will help, too. Wood chips, ash, dirt, sand, cat litter, leaves or almost anything is better than using nothing. Remember to use a lid to reduce the smell and spills. Last, a bucket toilet seat may prove useful.[83]

Alternatives and Supplements

If you're afraid things won't get back to normal soon, then using buckets and digging holes regularly isn't workable. Instead, consider building a latrine or an outhouse. Doing so will be more work initially, but the effort will pay off over the long-term. There are many designs if you'll only search YouTube, but the general idea is the same as when using buckets—separate urine and fecal matter, and layer with something organic between use.

Last, they make DIY composting toilets with urine diverters if you prefer, or you could even make one, though I don't suggest purchasing anything like this right now.[84] Focus on your plan for the short-term and consider what you'll do if things get worse, such as by constructing an outhouse. Remember to stock plenty of toilet paper, hand soap, and sanitizer, as mentioned previously.

Stoves and Cooking

Cooking food isn't solely about the comfort of eating a warm meal before bedtime. Properly cooked food is very much linked to your health. For instance, we all know by now that consuming undercooked meat or seafood can make you sick. But did you know that some vegetables, such as leafy greens and potatoes, can carry E. coli and salmonella? Eggs are ripe breeding grounds for salmonella, too. Even raw flour can make you ill.

How will you cook food or boil water if the power is out? What if the electric grid is unreliable or too expensive for you to rely on it any longer? I'm sure the trusty backyard BBQ grill will suffice for a while, but at some point, even the propane and charcoal briquettes will run out. It's time to get creative.

Perhaps the simplest solution is to cook food as we've done for millennia—over a campfire. The good news is that your campfire doesn't have to be rip-roaring to cook most foods. In fact, it's better to keep fires as minimal as possible to preserve fuel. The fact is that most campfires are highly inefficient. Instead, you're much better off containing a fire so that it's both more efficient and safer. And if you make a campfire, cook over the coals, not the fire.

It should go without saying, but I will anyway, that all open fires for any reason must be used outdoors, regardless of the weather and no matter how safe you believe you're being. The only exception would be when using an indoor wood stove for heating or cooking purposes.

The reason that open fires need to stay outdoors (where there's plenty of ventilation) isn't solely about a fire getting out of control and spreading indoors, but it's also about preventing carbon monoxide buildup, which can quickly become deadly. In fact, any device used for cooking or heating, such as a propane camping stove or propane space heater, that doesn't completely combust must always be used outdoors for this very reason.

Your safety is nothing to gloss over. As a result, I strongly encourage you to purchase enough carbon monoxide detectors to cover each level of your home and the garage at the bare minimum.[85] Smoke alarms and fire extinguishers are equally important, if not more so. Ensure these crucial safety items are in place, checked regularly (at least twice a year when we adjust clocks), and are immediately replaced if damaged or expired.

Back to alternative stove options. Perhaps the easiest DIY stove to create is the Hobo stove.[86] Simply take any #10 can and cut a rectangle out of the side, add several holes near the top to encourage proper aerodynamics of the fire, and that's about it. Remember to be careful, and use safety gloves, because you will cut metal, which can cut your skin easily if you slip.

A more efficient option than a basic hobo stove is the rocket stove.[87] People have made them out of many materials, me included. They've made them out of clay, concrete blocks, #10 cans, HVAC vent material, and even a 4x4 piece of lumber. I've made my fair share, too, including a vegetable can and tomato paste can years ago just to see if it was possible, and it worked better than I'd expected for how small it is.

Your imagination really is the limit here. Of course, there are plenty of commercial options available if you prefer. Search for the term *rocket stove* on Amazon and you'll find a wide range of choices. I won't attempt to mention every potential DIY stove people have made. Search YouTube and you'll find plenty to perk your interest.

I do, however, want to point out a wonderful option that we all should take advantage of—the solar oven—which uses only the power of the sun to cook food. They work great in the summer, decently in the spring and fall, and not so well in the winter, though this only partly depends on your latitude (because of the relative angle of the sun). In my experience, the decreased efficacy of a solar oven during the winter has more to do with general overcast or semi-cloudy conditions, as well as rain and snow, than it does with anything else. Your results may vary.

Please don't let sub-optimal performance during the winter dissuade you. Even during less than ideal times, a solar oven can be used to:

- Boil water to make it safe to drink. Because water only needs to reach 212 degrees Fahrenheit for a minute to become safe, you can use a solar oven to passively treat water while you attend to other activities. Interestingly, pasteurization temperatures of 135-162 degrees Fahrenheit are even easier to achieve. If this interests you, buy a WAPI indicator—a small device that contains wax which melts at a specific temperature.[88]

- Preheat water for bathing and sanitation purposes. Nobody enjoys a cold shower, which makes this an easy decision. Although there are other ways to passively heat water for bathing, such as by leaving a garden hose out in the sun for a few hours, a solar oven can easily accomplish this task, too. Just be sure the water isn't too hot before use so you don't burn your skin. Just mix in cold water until satisfactory.

- Warm shelf-stable food, such as canned soups or stews. There's no need to fire up the BBQ or start a campfire to heat already cook food when a solar oven can do it for you.

And those are just a few uses besides actually cooking food. Seeing as though a commercially made solar oven can reach temperatures of 400 degrees Fahrenheit with little trouble in direct sunlight, it will easily achieve the above uses, even in less than ideal conditions. Personally, I've made plenty of meals in our sun oven, from soups and fish to pizza and cobblers.[89] If food can fit inside, then you can probably cook it. And as you might suspect, there are plenty of alternative solar oven designs to choose from on Amazon, along with dozens of DIY ideas.[90] Here's an example of a solar oven I made mostly from two large boxes, shredded paper, and a sun visor.

If you're desperate, or not in a hurry, you could also place already cooked food on the dashboard of an enclosed vehicle on a sunny day. It will warm up food well-enough most of the time, though the inside of your vehicle may continuously smell like lunch.

If you're expecting to cook food and boil water outdoors, such as over a campfire, you'll soon discover that traditional pots and pans just won't hold up to the abuse. Instead, I encourage you to purchase cast iron cookware. But if you're not sure if you'll ever use it all, then focus solely on a cast iron Dutch oven, which is essentially a cast iron stock pot and lid, because you can cook almost anything in one.[91] A Dutch oven can even replicate oven-cooking when charcoal briquettes are added atop the lid.

Realize, too, that cooking over a campfire differs from a stovetop, in so much as you're more likely to burn food, especially if you're not paying attention. With that in mind, practice campfire cooking now or risk eating burned or undercooked food when you can least afford to do so.

Also, remember to purchase a lid lifter and a good pair of oven gloves so you don't burn yourself.[92] Last, so long as you properly care for your cast iron cookware (search YouTube for cleaning and seasoning), it will last a lifetime.

Alternatives and Supplements

If you're going to be starting a lot of fires for cooking, heating water, or whatever, then you're going to want plenty of matches and lighters, and maybe lighter fluid, too. While you could opt for the cheapest strike-on-box matches, I prefer long reach matches for ease of use. Purchase several boxes and store them where they won't get wet. You could also seal matches using a vacuum sealer for added protection, but it's unnecessary. Long neck lighters are an easy-to-use option as well. Ferro rods or a magnesium fire starter are a possibility, but they will take some practice to use properly.

As you might suspect, there are many creative ways to start a fire without matches or a lighter, such as by polishing the underside of a soda can or using steel wool and a 9-volt battery, but many DIY options leave a lot to be desired in the ease of use category. Stick with what works but know how to start a fire via other means if necessary.

Sterno cans deserve a special mention here because most of us have used them before. They store well, and canned fuel like this is an easy way to heat food, even indoors, when it's bitter-cold out.

Paper goods are the last thing I'll mention regarding cooking and eating. Paper goods, such as plates, bowls, and napkins are useful to include for disaster preparedness purposes because they reduce water usage since they don't need cleaned and make great fire-starters when you're done.

Of all the problems you'll be confronted with, cooking food is one of the easiest to fix, though you may need to be creative. Just remember never to do anything that could be dangerous, such as using an outdoor stove or BBQ indoors—even if partially ventilated—or leaving a fire unattended, and you'll be in good shape.

Entertainment

Nearly all forms of entertainment are directly tied to a functioning power grid these days. And, although everyone may be busier than usual, life without our expected forms of entertainment may be a rough transition for some of us, notably children. To help keep everyone happy, I encourage you to stock up on a variety of entertainment options.

Start with the most obvious choice—a deck of cards or two. Purchase a book of family card games and you'll have plenty of entertainment options to choose from right there.[93]

Fiction books are wonderful options, too. I can sometimes find these dirt cheap during local book store clearance sales and elsewhere. Or put it out on Facebook that you're looking for some freebies and maybe a friend will give you a starter library.

If you have young children, I suggest an assortment of classic board games, including Candy Land, Chutes and Ladders, and Operation. Monopoly, Clue, Sorry, and Scrabble are excellent alternatives for older children and adults.

A multi game set that includes chess, checkers, backgammon, and more is another great choice for the entire family, and one I highly recommend.[94]

Manual Tools

I know people who have collected more tools over their lifetime than most people would know what to do with, as well as those who don't even own a hammer. I know people who can build a house with just what they have on their tool belt, and others who couldn't hang a picture on a wall if their life depended on it. Where do you fall on that spectrum? I don't know. But I can say is that it's awfully difficult to drill a hole without a drill bit, pound a nail without a hammer, or drive a screw without a screwdriver. Basic tools make otherwise difficult, yet sometimes necessary, tasks a breeze.

Just think about what you would do if, for instance, your home was damaged during a storm and you had to board up a window to keep the wind out. You'll likely need a hammer and nails or a drill and screws to get it done properly. Or maybe you'll have to patch a leaky roof, which means a ladder would come in handy. Or perhaps it's getting cold out and, because of inflation, it's becoming prohibitively expensive to heat your home, so you decide to build a few passive solar heaters to help heat your home using only the power of the sun. Here, you may need quite a few tools, such as a handsaw, caulk gun, and drill bits.

Who knows what other tasks you may encounter. It would, therefore, be wise to keep a basic set of tools on hand. While it may be possible to borrow what you need from a friend or neighbor, I prefer to be as self-reliant as I can be. Now, because tools make so many tasks easier, have so many potential uses, and will last a lifetime—if they're of decent quality—that I encourage you to at least have the basics.

Basic Hand Tools

The following basic hand tools and related items could prove useful to you down the road, including:

- Claw Hammer
- Crowbar
- Handsaw (for cutting wood)
- Hacksaw (for basic metal cuts)
- Tape measure
- Pliers (e.g., slip-joint, locking, needle-nose)
- Screwdriver set (Phillips and flat heads)
- Wrench set (in SAE and metric)
- Allen wrench set and torx/star key set
- Caulk gun
- Utility knife
- Tin snips (for thin metal cuts)
- Wood chisel set
- Level
- Clamps (e.g. bar or spring style)
- Ladder, 6 foot or taller

I'll include a lengthier list in Appendix C, if interested.

What About Power Tools?

Power tools make many laborious repair and construction tasks far easier, few more so than the typical hand drill. Most are cordless these days, but corded drills have their place, too. And if times get truly hard, a manual hand drill may find use.[95] Remember to include a drill bit set and screwdriver bit set, or most drills will turn into paperweights rather quickly.

A circular saw can be quite useful, too, as are a variety of other power tools, like a reciprocating saw, but if you don't already have—and use—these types of tools around the house, then there's little reason to mention specifics beyond a drill and circular saw.

There's no need to get fancy or pay a lot of money for power tools, as even hand tools will get the job done eventually. That said, if you have nothing now, look in your local classified ads or on Facebook marketplace for garage or estate sales where you'll sometimes find people all but giving such things away. It just takes a bit of patience.

I would be remiss if I failed to mention safety gear. Working with tools can be dangerous, particularly if you're inexperienced. Be sure to include multiple pairs of safety glasses, ear protection, and work gloves, at minimum. A hard hat and respirator may be in order as well. There are a variety of additional safety items which could prove useful, though many are only intended for specific tools, such as chaps for chainsaws or a welder's mask for welding. Stick with the basics for now, then expand as necessary.

Additional Manual Tools to Consider

Basic hand tools and power tools are only scratching the surface of what may prove useful to you during hard times, but I don't know your situation. You may live in an apartment complex and find none of the following necessary. I have a budding homestead with dozens of trees, a vegetable garden, chickens, along with more animals and projects on the way. Because I use gardening tools and even construction tools regularly, I'll find need to include these items in my must-have list, so much so that I have duplicates where possible.

- Gardening tools: round and flat shovels, scoop, spade, rake, hoe, mattock, handheld shovels, wheelbarrow, or garden cart, scythe, or billhook.
- Woodworking tools: axe, hatchet, splitting maul, wood splitting wedge, file set.
- Construction/demolition tools: hand auger, post hole digger, sledgehammer, ripping bar.

Again, most of the aforementioned items are so useful that I have backups, notably extra shovels, rakes, and axes. And, as you might suspect, it's quite difficult for others to pitch on extensive projects if you only have one tool to get the job done.

In addition, tools break and dull. Therefore, I suggest that you (1) have some ability to repair tools, such as by purchasing extra handles for shovels and axes, and (2) can sharpen blades and edges. Handheld metal files are helpful here, though an electric angle grinder is faster.

Alternatives and Supplements

All the tools in the world will do you no good if you're missing crucial supplies. Nails and screws are obvious examples, though there are many additional items which could prove useful, such as a variety of nuts and bolts, duct tape, glues, caulking, foam insulation, epoxy, and even lubricants, like WD-40. Vaseline is great for a variety of survival uses, too, including as a lubricant, to aid with fire-starting, lip balm, wound care, and so much more.

In addition, supplies necessary for construction or, more likely, repairing your home are something to consider. This could also involve electrical wiring, copper pipe, PVC pipe, PEX tubing, plywood, and assorted lumber, to name several other examples. You'll want to include the tools and supplies required to make use of these items, should it come to that. For instance, PVC pipe will need PVC cement and probably an assortment of fittings to be of use; PEX tubing requires specialized fittings, too, as well as a special crimping tool; household wiring requires special connectors and tools as well.

WARNING: There's also a fair bit of knowledge required to perform home repairs properly and safely. Although a quality home repair book will help the novice a lot—and often provide suitable safety warnings—ignorance can be deadly. If you're at all unsure of what you're doing, find someone who knows. In fact, I strongly encourage you to identify those who have such specialized knowledge, such as a retired neighbor. Make friends now and consider how you might reciprocate should you ever actually need their help.

Tarps

Tarps are a very useful item to stock up on as times get tough because they have so many quick and easy uses around the house. Several of the more obvious ones include as a makeshift shelter for people or animals, ground cover, to patch a broken window or hole in the roof, to keep firewood dry, and to protect garden vegetables and fruit trees during times of frost.

If you'd like to get more creative, tarps can be used:

- As a makeshift awning, thus reducing sunlight and heat penetration into your home.
- To collect rainwater, which will probably be much cleaner than anything collected off a rooftop or via groundwater sources.
- As a component of blackout shades, which keeps light from leaking out through windows and doors.
- As an "envelope" of sorts to protect a sleeping bag from getting wet.

If you're desperate, tarps can be ripped into thin strips to create cordage for lashings, can be fashioned like a bag to carry supplies, and can be transformed into a poncho if need be. But these are uses much better performed by other gear. My advice is to keep tarps whole and in-tact as much as possible.

Purchase Recommendations

Tarp sizes between 6'x8' and 20'x30' should suffice for most scenarios, but tarps (1) get exponentially more expensive the larger they are, and (2) vary in relative quality. Stick to purchasing tarps between 6'x8' and 10'x12' to save on money because these sizes are the most commonly available on the market. Besides, if you need something larger, you can always lash tarps together.

Tarp quality is vitally important. Avoid anything labeled lightweight, as they never last through any significant use. Heavy-duty tarps are preferable, though medium-duty tarps should suffice for most uses if cost is a major concern. Tarps should have eyelets (or grommets) so you can more easily attach cordage to them. And if they're labeled as rip-stop, then that's best, but not a deal-breaker. Specific colors may be useful, such as using brown or camo tarps in a wooded area to hide something, but it's not crucial.

How many tarps you should purchase is hard to say. A handful would be a good start if you don't currently foresee using many right now. As time and money permit, add a few more.

Last, it's wise to include plenty of cordage in order to make use of your tarps because they'll often be secured to structures, each other, or a tree, which is difficult to do without rope. Many preppers prefer paracord, but anything that's relatively sturdy should suffice for most uses that I can foresee. That said, relying on twine may not be the best option. Purchase a few to several hundred feet of something sturdy, like paracord, and you should have plenty to see you through most scenarios. Remember to melt the ends to keep the cordage from fraying.

Alternatives and Supplements

Plastic sheeting can be used similarly to tarps sometimes, but they're much more prone to rips and punctures, so you'll need to be more careful when using them in place of tarps. That said, plastic sheeting can certainly waterproof almost anything, can collect rainwater, transform into a solar still, cover firewood or a vegetable garden, and become a makeshift poncho.[96] Plastic sheeting can also be useful for creating a makeshift quarantine room or for sheltering-in-place applications as well. If you must choose between clear or black plastic, choose clear as it has more survival applications than black does.

Large contractor-sized garbage bags can be nearly as useful as tarps, since they can also collect water, function as a poncho, blackout windows, keep gear dry, and transform into an emergency tube tent to name a few ideas. And of course, they're great for containing trash that may accumulate after a disaster. Keep a few boxes around, just in case.

Buckets

If tarps are useful to stockpile, buckets are a must-have because we can use them for a variety of purposes, including:

- Long-term food storage;
- Containing supplies for ease of movement (such as in a bug out situation);
- Temporary toilet;
- Haul and/or store water or other liquid;
- Growing food (known as bucket gardening);
- Makeshift laundry wash system;
- Wring out clothes after being washed;
- Create a Big Berkey clone water filter
- Biosand filter;
- Cache equipment (can be buried);
- Hide supplies inside the house (a five gallon paint bucket should be overlooked by all but the most zealous thief);
- Homemade A/C (needs ice and a fan);
- Animal feeder;
- Mouse trap.

Most of the ideas mentioned above require permanently modifying a bucket, such as by drilling holes, so you'll want to consider how you might use them in order to avoid modifying every bucket.

There are plenty of other ideas for buckets, plenty of which I'll likely never use, such as building material and exercise equipment (when filled with something like dirt or sand). The point in mentioning these ideas is to get you thinking about how such an otherwise mundane item as a bucket can prove even more useful to you during hard times.

Stick with the ubiquitous five- or six-gallon buckets as the most useful options. Food-grade buckets aren't absolutely necessary, but they are preferable for storing food or water for later consumption.

As far as how many buckets to purchase, I'd say a dozen buckets along with a handful of food-grade buckets should suffice for most projects. Remember lids, too.

Personally, I have dozens of buckets in various states of use and modification. They'll last a lifetime if even remotely cared for, stack easily, and will be worth their weight in gold during hard times.

Alternatives and Supplements

There are a variety of containers and boxes around most homes that could be fashioned into a makeshift bucket—just look around your home—but few items will function as easily as a basic bucket. Buckets are inexpensive now. Grab several while you still can.

Books

I'm sure you've heard the phrase "knowledge is power," but few people realize just how much free knowledge we have available in today's world. We all know that a simple search on YouTube will explain how to do nearly anything. Books, like this one, can be downloaded to a computer in mere seconds, and a smartphone can search the internet to your heart's content.

Aside from localized problems, such as regular brownouts, or personal problems, like being unable to afford to pay the electric bill if you lose your job, maybe entire companies declare bankrupt and can no longer afford to maintain their many servers. Or, maybe, in order to pay their bills, companies charge for access to information that was once freely available because their advertising revenues have fallen off a cliff. Or maybe we get to where printed materials reign supreme again, but you wind up priced out of the market because other people can afford to pay more. I don't know the exact reason. What I can say is that information is dirt cheap right now relative to its potential usefulness in the future. But there's an easy way and a hard way to gather such knowledge.

Nearly two decades ago, when I first became interested in preparedness, I spent countless hours downloading, printing, and organizing loads of survival information. It was new to me, and I wanted everything I could get my hands on. I had binders of papers on my bookshelves, and I was proud of my efforts, but there was a problem. I never read most of what I'd printed out. Truth be told, I eventually tossed all of that information in favor of books I later purchased, some books of which I also haven't fully read through. In my defense, several of the books I keep are solely for reference, such as canning recipe books or medical information, while others are acted upon now, such as the information presented here.

Recommended Books to Purchase

Focus on purchasing books that teach skills you don't already have or which require specific knowledge that is easy to forget, such as canning recipes.

This should include books about country living, homesteading, living off-grid, canning, preserving food, and medical knowledge as the primary concerns. You may also want to include books which discuss more primitive skills, such as bushcraft skills, wilderness survival, and edible and medicinal plants, to name a few. Home repair books may be of use, too. Really, anything that explains how to do something which benefits your survival and ability to get things done on your own is great to have on hand. I'll include a more thorough reference in Appendix D. For now, I highly recommend the following books to start:

- *The Encyclopedia of Country Living* by Carla Emery;
- *Back to Basics* by Abigail Gehring;
- *The Survival Medicine Handbook*, 3rd edition by Dr. Joseph Alton;
- *Ball Complete Book of Home Preserving* by Judi Kingry;
- *Bushcraft 101* by Dave Canterbury.

While print books are best, e-books are acceptable if cost is a concern. Download e-books to a trusty e-reader or laptop computer, and ensure you can keep it charged using an off-grid power source if the electrical grid goes out, is unreliable, or becomes too expensive to use.

Alternatives and Supplements

If you absolutely cannot afford a survival library, even an electronic version, then I recommend you look for free information online just as I did all those years ago. If you need a place to start, I keep an ongoing database of survival and preparedness resources on my website.[97] You'll find free information covering a wide range of survival topics, including food storage and cooking, medical guides, personal safety, water procurement and treatment, and plenty more. It's all free, and many of the more important references are already PDF files that can be easily downloaded.

If you want even more resources than what I offer, then I suggest you search online for "survival PDF files" or something similar. When you do, you'll encounter sites like SeasonedCitizenPrepper.com which have compiled links to a wide range of PDF files that may be of use.[98] I will caution you, however, that it's easy to become overwhelmed by such information and, as a result, never take action.

Ultimately, if you're going to go the route of downloading PDF files for later reference, be sensible about what you download and absolutely about what you print. I will also mention that you should be wary about where you get your information, particularly online, as some of it could be outdated, incomplete, or flat-out wrong. And if you're unsure about what you read, verify with other sources.

Last, there may come a time when computers and keyboards no longer function, so you'll have to go back to paper and pencil to create lists for yourself, leave instructions for others, or journal your thoughts for future generations to name a few uses. You can often find spiral-bound notebooks or pads of paper inexpensively around the time of back-to-school sales. Include plenty of #2 pencils, a pencil sharpener, and several erasers to round things out. Permanent markers are useful for labeling purposes.

Off-Grid Power

We've talked extensively about ways to survive without grid power, and how to cope with expensive or unreliable power generation. Know that you don't have to be at the mercy of the power company. You can generate your own power fairly easily, but it's going to cost you. Let's start with something I don't recommend: whole-house power.

Expect to pay upwards of twenty-thousand dollars for the average whole-house solar installation. That's not horrible considering just how important power is to our lives, but there's a big problem most people don't think about—the expectation that you'll have a functional electric grid to act as a battery bank. Even a whole-house solar system won't be useful if the power grid goes down.

Other problems with all solar systems include less power generation in cloudy conditions (and during the winter months when the sun is low in the sky), zero power generation at night, routine maintenance (e.g., removing dust or snow accumulation from the panels), and dealing with shady or disreputable solar panel salespeople.

But let's focus on the fundamental problem—no battery bank—because it's crucial to keeping the electricity flowing. Solar panels do a great job of generating power, but what they can't do is regulate that power to the devices which need it, such as a refrigerator, microwave, or laptop. You'll need a steady source of power to do that; deep-cycle batteries are the solution. Now, there's more to a proper off-grid system than panels and batteries, but you need to understand that the batteries alone can cost as much as, if not more than, the panels, which could expand that twenty-thousand dollar investment into a forty- or fifty-thousand dollar one quickly.

Most of us can't afford to spend that much on an off-grid system, I know I can't, so we do the next best thing: buy something much smaller, then prioritize and ration power. For me, that ended up being a few thousand watt system capable of powering crucial appliances, particularly a full-sized refrigerator and chest freezer, along with a few other items for years without concern. If rationed, I could use the system to operate power tools and other small appliances, like a window air-conditioning unit, when needed. High-consumption devices, like the toaster, coffee pot, and microwave, are simply going to collect a lot of dust if things got that desperate.

The intricacies of off-grid power can be complex, so I'll point you toward the person who's advice I ended up following: Will Prowse of Mobile-SolarPower.com.[99]

But even developing a small setup like what I suggest can feel overwhelming. Instead, consider a solar generator, such as those made by Bluetti, Goal Zero or Jackery. They take the guesswork out solar power by incorporating everything you need in one package besides the solar panels, which are usually solar separately. Solar generators are portable, often expendable, and quite reliable. Although you will pay a bit more for the convenience, if you merely want to ensure your refrigerator keeps running when the power goes out for a very long time, buy a quality solar generator along with their recommended panels and you'll be set.

This is a good time to mention a traditional fuel-powered generator. These typically run on gasoline, though some generators are powered with diesel, propane, natural gas, or some combination of the above. Although useful for short-term emergencies, unless you expect having the ability to refuel them over the duration of whatever is to come, I don't recommend them for this application.

Perhaps the only exception would be a generator connected to a large propane tank of, say, one-thousand gallons or more. But this setup gets expensive quickly. That said, if you already have a large propane tank on your property, then it may be an option to consider. Personally, I would rather buy more solar panels and batteries for a truly long-term, off-grid solution. As with most things, this is about tradeoffs. Do you want less power over a longer period (as with solar panels), or more power now (via a fuel-powered generator)?

Alternatives and Supplements

Realize, too, that off-grid solar is only one option. Small wind turbines are often a fantastic supplement to solar and are something I'm considering adding soon. Missouri Wind and Solar is a wonderful resource for both solar and wind, including hybrid systems—those that incorporate both wind and solar in one setup.[100]

A pedal generator—a device you literally pedal to produce power—is another option for those who just have to get their workout in, even during the worst of times. It's not for me, but if you're going to exercise anyway, you may as well charge batteries.

No doubt there are plenty of other resources online, and countless YouTube videos. But you have to be careful where you get your advice from as you could easily spend thousands of dollars on equipment that may not be right for your situation or climate, or is incompatible with other components.

Miscellaneous Items to Stockpile

The following selection of items is in no particular order. It includes gear and supplies that didn't quite require a full discussion of their own, but which may still be useful for you to have.

Fishing Gear

Sourcing food, from any source possible, should be in the back of your mind at all times. Fishing, a time-honored tradition, is one great way to procure food that almost anyone can do. Fishing can be slow-paced and isn't always easy, but it's not like you're having to chase down a gazelle in the middle of the savannah either.

I'm not much of an angler, but so long as you have the basics—rod and reel, line, tackle, bait—then fishing is a possibility.

When, where, and how you'll go about fishing will depend on where you live, but if this interests you, then find someone who fishes nearby and ask them for advice. It might surprise you to find many local fishing spots nearby, some of which you didn't even know existed. There are also useful smartphone apps that can point you in the right direction if you don't know anyone who can help.[101]

Pest Control Supplies

During normal times, pests, like ants, cockroaches, and flies, are a mere nuisance. Maybe you'll get out some bug spray and deal with the problem yourself. Or sometimes it's worse than that and you have to call in an exterminator. Problem solved. But, and I suspect you see this coming by now, how bad might infestations get when the sewer system stops functioning or your trash isn't being taken away? Or maybe you're cooking outside regularly and leaving a mess behind? And what if your neighbors make things harder somehow, such as by not burying their excrements?

We toe a fine line during normal times regarding keeping insects, rodents, and wildlife at bay. Infestations will only worsen if any part of our modern infrastructure falters for a significant length of time. You should, therefore, have some ability to manage the most common pests in your area. This should include an assortment of traps, sprays, and prevention options. Focus on the main problem insects in your area, though most everyone has trouble with ants, cockroaches, spiders and flies at some point. Other problem bugs include mosquitoes, termites, wasps and bed bugs.

Wildlife can become a real problem, too, notably rats, mice, racoons, and even deer, though there are many other candidates depending on where you live. Again, consider the wildlife in your area and realize that they will probably encroach on your land more than normal if given an incentive.

There are many DIY methods for treating and managing pests if you prefer not to use harsh chemicals or traps. Dawn dish soap, for instance, boasts several alternative uses, including for pest and weed control. Borax is great for managing a variety of insects as well. You can create a makeshift mousetrap, wasp trap, and fly trap. And then there are common sense ways to manage both insects and wildlife, like promptly burying garbage, not leaving food scraps lying around when eating, and cleaning dishes after use, to name a few of the more obvious solutions. Search online and you'll find many additional recommendations.

Communication Equipment

It's likely that you're accustomed to receiving your news from social media platforms or network cable. But there could come a time where your favorite news platform shuts down or becomes inaccessible for whatever reason. Having a trusty radio on hand may, as a result, become indispensable in your ability to gather pressing information from across the country, even abroad.

I suggest a basic battery-operated shortwave radio. These radios almost always receive AM and FM bands as well, and because they're designed to receive shortwave frequencies, can receive transmissions from around the world.

Whatever radio you opt for doesn't need any fancy gimmicks, like Bluetooth, and it doesn't even need to have digital tuning, though that can be helpful. And while you can get a usable shortwave radio for less than a hundred dollars right now, most decent options are going to cost more than that.

Two-way radios, commonly referred to as walkie talkies or FRS radios, are another potentially useful communication device for around the house or when traveling in a caravan. Ensure that any two-way radio you choose can use AA or AAA alkaline batteries rather than a proprietary battery that needs to be charged via cord or which cannot be replaced. Remember to include extra batteries because two-way radios use up batteries fast.

There are other communication options available, such as GMRS and HAM radio, but these require special knowledge and licensing, and even specialized equipment, so I wouldn't put my money here.

Last, there are smartphone apps for tuning in radio stations, even stations abroad, but they will require functional cell towers, so here we are again relying on big businesses and the power grid. You how where I stand on that.

Fruit Trees, Berry Bushes, and Vegetable Seeds

Even stockpiling shelf-stable food and planting a large vegetable garden might not be enough if the country gets as bad as some fear. Having food that replenishes year after year is always a good idea. Fruit trees and berry bushes do just that. Of course, not all fruits grow well in some climates, so visit a local nursery for advice if you know little about it.

Realize, however, that saplings often take years to grow into a tree large enough to produce fruit. Berry bushes and vines often produce fruit much more quickly. Some, like blackberries, spread and grow all on their own. Others, like blueberries, need more care. Many can propagate to become new bushes. Fruits and berries provide a good amount of vitamins and nutrients and are a tasty treat. I encourage you to grow something.

Vegetable seeds are a necessity for growing a garden. Sadly, most of us amateur gardeners purchase new seeds each year because we don't know any better. Although true that seeds lose some efficacy with each passing year of storage, it is possible to save seeds each season and not have that problem.[102] It's fairly easy, but saving seeds requires some effort and proper timing. Do your research so you know when to harvest seeds, how to dry them, and how to store them properly. The *Seed Saving Bible* by Remo Gentry is a place to start.[103]

119

Gas Cans and Fuel Stabilizers

Gasoline and diesel may be in short supply for years to come or merely erratic in availability. At the very least, stockpile enough fuel in five-gallon gas cans, treated with a fuel stabilizer, such as PRI-G (for gasoline) or PRI-D (for diesel), to fill a gas tank full for evacuation as well as those times when gasoline is scarce and you absolutely must travel.

You might also buy more fuel stabilizer to keep on hand for future use. Not only can it be used to store gasoline for longer periods, but it can sometimes revitalize stale gas.

Realize that, while storing fuel in approved containers is safe if done properly, sometimes it's dangerous, such as storing gasoline near an open flame or in an unventilated area.[104] Storing a lot of gasoline, say, over ten or twenty gallons, may even be against city or county ordinances or other regulatory bodies. Always choose to store fuel wisely and safely.

Manual Kitchen Tools

It never hurts to have a few handheld kitchen tools in case the power goes out. For instance, a manual can opener is a must-have backup tool I suggest everyone has, especially considering all the shelf-stable canned foods I expect you to purchase. Other useful handheld kitchen implements include: an egg beater, whisk, potato masher, and cheese grater. You could take it a step further and buy items like a manual pasta maker or meat grinder, but that might be a bit much to start with.

Manual Knife Sharpener

My guess is that you have plenty of knives around the kitchen and possibly elsewhere. You might also have an electric knife sharpener, which is great because they get the job done fast. But they don't work without power, and because knives are useful for a variety of survival-related tasks, it's wise to include a manual knife sharpener.

Handheld Cleaning Tools

Whereas I'd mentioned cleaning supplies in part one, I didn't suggest handheld cleaners. I'm specifically thinking of items like a broom and dust pan, mop and bucket, scrub brushes, sponges, and rags. A manual carpet and floor sweeper may be of use, too. Really, anything that can replace their electrical-counterparts is good to consider.

Spare Parts, Chemicals

I've mentioned previously how tools break, but parts for useful equipment (e.g., chainsaws, tillers) and vehicles wear out, too, no matter how careful we are when using them. For example, spark plugs, air filters, belts, and chains must all be replaced at some point.

Engine oil gets dirty. Coolant may need replaced. Chainsaws need bar oil. You get the idea.

Although some items can be cleaned to an extent, most spare parts and basic chemicals are inexpensive, all things considered. Look at the equipment you own and consider what you cannot be without, then determine precisely which spare parts and chemicals you'll need to stockpile to keep them running.

A further note regarding chemicals: There are many other sprays and lubes that I haven't mentioned, many of which could prove valuable in the right circumstance. For instance, penetrating oil—useful for removing stuck bolts—isn't the same as a typical lubricant. There are different lubricants, such as silicone sprays, dry lubes, lithium grease, special oil for firearms, and plenty more. I'm not saying you'll absolutely need any of these specialty chemicals, but mechanical items tend to function a lot better when they're in proper working order. Chemicals, such as those mentioned above, help make that happen.

Additional Considerations

Following are several more topics we need to discuss, albeit briefly, because they're less about what to buy and more about what to consider from now on.

Extra Mouths to Feed

I've hinted at this concern once or twice already, but it bears further mention. Whether you choose to take in others is up to you. If you do, I sure hope they're expected to help in exchange for your generosity. That said, having extra hands around could be beneficial to you, too. No doubt aging slows us down, me included, and even prevents us from doing things we once accomplished with ease.

Having extra supplies on hand, and by that I mean purchasing even more than what I recommend or what you believe you'll need, never hurts. Honestly, there's no harm in stockpiling two or three times what I suggest—of almost any resource—if you can afford to do so. Not only does this provide a buffer for the hardest of times, but it also allows for you take in additional people, like friends or friends, without them becoming a burden. This strategy even allows for charity toward neighbors or anyone down on their luck.

Of course, I don't want you to spend every last dime, just in case. Stockpile as money and resources allow.

Stockpiling Specifically for Barter

At some point, you may have considered buying more supplies for barter, and I wouldn't blame you. But I don't think it's a wise investment, in part because you could spend that money on other items and supplies you might use, but also because you're opening yourself up for trouble. Remember that if most people aren't prepared at all, but now you're offering them something truly useful, such as food or medicine, in exchange for what little they may have left, well, that's a recipe for disaster.

Granted, I can envision a world where, after things have settled down, that a barter economy could become commonplace. It's natural and will assuredly be welcomed by most. But that scenario is a long way down the road. Chances are that you will have used up a large portion of anything you might stockpile specifically for barter. And if you can afford to purchase vast quantities of items specifically for barter, reach out to me... I'd like to move into your basement. I know a lot, so it'll work out. I promise.

Addressing Health Problems

It's easy to put off having health concerns addressed, but if we assume that our medical system may not function properly for some time and you have things you're putting off, health considerations should be top of the list. This could include almost anything, from eye surgery to dental work, getting your back fixed, or hangnail surgery. If it's bothering you and could become a problem during hard times, I suggest you seek proper medical care and get it taken care of. No doubt there are health troubles that will crop up, and other concerns that aren't able to be corrected, but for everything else, now's the time.

Living in an Apartment, Condominium, or City

I won't lie to you. Survival will be difficult enough for the average suburban homeowner, even with this list in hand. But also trying to survive while living in an apartment or condo, or Heaven-forbid, in a major city, will be a nightmare because you'll have far more people to contend with, and considerably fewer resources to rely upon.

Security will be a primary concern day and night. Sourcing water will be exceedingly difficult. Diseases will thrive because of a lack of functioning sewers, no garbage disposal, and malnutrition. And even if you don't live in a major city, the logistics of living in an apartment complex or condominium where the vast majority of tenants are likely unprepared is problematic, to say the least. After all, one can only keep their level of preparedness under wraps for so long, I'm afraid.

These are not trivial concerns. More people living near you raise the chances of trouble substantially,

125

especially when they become desperate. And if you're the only person who has something—anything—they might need for themselves or their family, then that will only spell trouble for you.

Very few of us will avoid such trouble. To an extent, I live out in the country, but I suspect it won't take long for the unprepared masses to flee cities, even smaller ones like the city I live near, looking for anything they might consume.

Most cities offer very few useful resources once supply chains fail. They will become death traps. Move while you can or find someone or somewhere that you might evacuate to. But even this, I'm afraid, isn't easy or cheap. Consider such a move carefully.

For what it's worth, I once wrote a book about small space prepping, such as in an apartment or condo, but it's really about prepping with minimal space, and less about how to survive during a collapse.[105] Either way, I'm happy to share it with you. Just send me an email, damian@rethinksurvival.com, tell me that you've read this book, and I'll happily send you a copy via email.

Form a Group or Lone Wolf?

For the longest time, I would've considered myself a lone wolf prepper. I often preferred doing things myself, including my preparations. But that's when I was younger. Now that I'm older, and the more my back hurts, the more value I find in having help whenever I can get it.

But this isn't solely about having someone help me weed the garden or dig holes for an outhouse. It's really about specialized knowledge and someone having my back when times get really hard.

Even though I've been working towards being better prepared for nearly a decade now, there's still so much I don't know. Knowledge that I will honestly never have. For instance, my eldest son is a plumber's apprentice. He already knows more about plumbing than I ever will. My in-laws know more about canning than I do, and my father-in-law is the resident expert gardener. My wife is a nurse. I also know people who can hunt and fish with the best of them. The list goes on. This is, whether or not others realize it, indirectly forming a prepper group because it brings together an array of knowledge—knowledge that I don't need to possess myself—for when times get tough. I suggest you consider who in your life possesses such expertise and bring them into the fold.

I also believe that forming a prepper group, even a loosely formed one, is about other people having your back. This is crucial because people are far less likely to help someone out if they don't first have a relationship with them. Of course, some relationships are inherently stronger than others, such as familial bonds, though merely knowing a person by name or face is better than nothing at all. Getting to know your neighbors is a great start. After all, you could meet a retired veteran, police officer, doctor, veterinarian, electrician, plumber, or even a lady who can sew anything together. They're all wonderful people to get to know... probably.

We all have skills and knowledge, but it's impossible to know everything. Reach out to those who have knowledge you don't and make friends. And consider what skills and knowledge you have to reciprocate with. That's the best way to form a relationship of all.

What to Focus on if Money is Tight

This is the million-dollar question, isn't it? After all, I've given you quite a list of items to consider, and if you had to purchase everything from scratch, well, that could cost a small fortune. And since most of us live paycheck to paycheck, this just isn't workable.

I suspect, however, that you have more resources than you realize, but you need to take stock in the event some items aren't in good working order. For instance, maybe you have some fishing gear, but you haven't looked through it in twenty years and now everything is a slimy, rusty ball of fishing line and lures. Or perhaps you have several tarps, but you have left them out in the weather for years and now they're a shredded mess. Or maybe the gasoline you have stored hasn't been properly treated, and now it's stale. You get the idea.

But let's say neglect isn't the case, and you only want to focus on buying supplies now while spending as little as possible. Here, the short answer is to focus on items listed in part one because they're what you'll most likely need right from the start and, better yet, will almost certainly be used down the road regardless of the coming hard times, so it won't feel as if you're spending money frivolously.

Food and hygiene supplies are the obvious places to start because they will be used up at some point, and it's likely that these supplies are as inexpensive as they're ever going to be. Because being well-fed is intricately linked to proper decision-making, and keeping clean is crucial to your health, I would focus most of my resources here if I had limited resources.

Dealing with minor health concerns, something I believe will become more prevalent during hard times, suggests that first aid supplies and medications are a must-have shortly thereafter. Even if you're not directly preventing a minor problem, such as a cut, from becoming a major one, feeling miserable isn't any fun either, which is precisely what most over-the-counter medications are useful for. And if you rely on prescription medications, discuss options with your doctor because these are likely the most important supplies to never run short of.

Whether you need more clothing, shoes, or additional glasses, and so on, is up to you. But I wouldn't ignore these crucial items if you have nothing to begin with since they can be absolutely necessary in the right circumstances. The same can be said for firearms and other self-defense items, too. But these items aren't cheap, so you'll want to be strategic about your purchases. For example, I might be more inclined to purchase a firearm before upgrading my home security because if somebody is that intent on getting inside, then I should expect real trouble.

Regarding the items in part two: It's much more difficult for me to pinpoint precisely what you might need. As I explained earlier, I use an assortment of tools, including garden tools, regularly, but you might rarely step foot outside and thus never need them.

Likewise, if the state of our supply chains and utilities never falters as I expect, you would probably never need tarps, buckets, stoves, off-grid power, or nearly anything on this list. But then that's the inherent risk of choosing to be prepared for what *might* come if it never does. Truth be told, many of the items detailed in part two are only necessary if hard times really strike the vast majority. But if that happens, you'll be forever thankful.

If you must restrict your purchases drastically, then consider:

- Limiting flashlight and lanterns to one or two each, and use them sparingly (still purchase plenty of batteries).
- A mini fridge may still prove useful, but look for a used option to save money.
- A box fan or two isn't expensive, and they're Heaven-sent during the summer's worst.
- Sleeping bags will help immensely if you're unable to heat your home.
- Buy the Sawyer Mini water filter and use two buckets to create a gravity filter instead of the more expensive Berkey filter.
- Buy a digging shovel so you can bury waste and garbage.
- Make your own solar oven.
- Limit entertainment to a deck of cards.
- Borrow tools from neighbors, but expect to repay them somehow.
- Buy a few lightweight tarps and cheap buckets, so you'll have something.
- Download eBooks instead of buying print copies, then hope the power never goes out.
- Develop a tiny off-grid power option since even a small setup can power a mini fridge or laptop.

Being frugal is challenging, but it's not impossible. Ask friends and neighbors if they have anything they're trying to get rid of that you might find useful. Alternatively, search your local Classified ads or Facebook Marketplace, as I've mentioned multiple times throughout, for deals. It might surprise you how many useful items people are selling at dirt cheap prices right now, or even giving away simply because they want it out of their house or garage.

Clearly, being frugal will take more time, but start now and you'll be that much more ahead of everyone else when they realize the crunch has hit.

Concluding Thoughts

I understand that you now have a lot to consider, especially if you're new to preparedness. But I won't sugarcoat reality either—even with these items in hand, life will probably be much harder for many of us when times truly get tough. Modern society makes life so easy, all things considered, that any transition away from its many conveniences will be a challenge. But they're not insurmountable challenges either.

On a positive note, society will return to normal at some point. I don't know how long that will take or what things will look like when we get there. I don't even know if we'll be a united nation or not at that point. What I know is that, with these many items at your disposal, you and your family will have a solid chance to make it through. But you must start now. Waiting until the late-night news announces, "We've collapsed!" is simply too late.

Remember, too, that going into debt or depleting your savings account isn't the right strategy either. That will only put undue stress on you and surely hinder your ability to prepare down the road. Spend money wisely, and take your time to do this properly because, while I don't see the U.S. Dollar collapsing overnight, the cracks are showing whether the powers that be want them to or not.

Last, if you're ever unsure what else you can do, reach out to me, damian@rethinksurvival.com. I'm happy to brainstorm and help.

Discover More Survival Books

If you liked what you read within, then you're going to love my other survival books.[106] Here's a sampling:

- *57 Scientifically Proven Survival Foods to Stockpile*
- *Crisis Preparedness Guide*
- *53 Essential Bug Out Bag Supplies*
- *28 Powerful Home Security Solutions*
- *47 Easy DIY Survival Projects*
- *27 Crucial Smartphone Apps for Survival*
- *The Get Home Bag and Compact EDC Kit*

And if you would like to be among the first to know when new survival books become available, fill out this form and you'll be notified via email.[107]

Recommended for You

I want to point out one book from the above list since you clearly understand the importance of preparing for what's coming: *Crisis Preparedness Guide: How to Survive the Coming Collapse.*

There's so much more you can and should do besides buying supplies. Click here to discover what every family must know, starting right now.[108]

Appendices

Appendix A: 101-Point Checklist

Appendix B: Food Storage Checklist

Appendix C: Hand Tools Checklist

Appendix D: Recommended Books

Appendix E: List of Resources

Appendix A: 101-Point Checklist

(Note: Items are listed in the order in which they were discussed, thus some items may appear out of place.)

PART 1: Items to Buy Now to See You Through the Initial Crisis

Shelf-Stable Foods

- Shelf-stable foods (canned meats, beans, vegetables, fruits; spaghetti and pasta sauce, dehydrated potatoes, packaged side dishes, cereals); see Appendix B for a complete list.
- Powdered baby formula, if needed.
- Dry pet food, as necessary.
- Bulk dry goods (rice, oats, spaghetti, macaroni, granola, pancake mix, dry beans).
- Seasonings (salt, pepper, cumin, chili powder, garlic powder, onion powder, oregano).
- Multivitamins.
- Electrolyte powder.

Hygiene and Cleaning Supplies

- Personal hygiene supplies (hand soap, bar soap, shampoo, conditioner, deodorant, toothpaste, floss, mouthwash, feminine hygiene products, shaving supplies, lotion, and hand sanitizer).
- Assorted household cleaners (dish soap, laundry soap, bathroom cleaners, floor and carpet

cleaners, household sprays of all sorts, spray disinfectants and wipes).

- Toilet paper, facial tissue, paper towels, and napkins.
- Garbage bags (both 13-gallon kitchen bags and 30-gallon or larger bags).
- Sunscreen.
- Bug spray.
- Additional household supplies (isopropyl alcohol, hydrogen peroxide, bleach, white vinegar, baking soda, borax, and ammonia).
- Supplies for children and infants, like diapers or pull-ups (will grow into larger sizes).

First Aid Supplies and Medications

- Wound care supplies (antibiotic ointment, a wide variety of bandages, plenty of sterile gauze pads and rolls, medical tape, elastic wrap, moleskin, and disposable gloves).
- OTC medications (pain meds, decongestants, antihistamines, antacids, antidiarrheals, laxatives, expectorants, topical analgesics, and topical steroids).
- Prescription medications, as necessary.
- Antibiotics?

Appropriate Clothing and Shoes

- Outdoor clothing appropriate for your climate (windbreaker/insulated jacket, insulated gloves,

stocking cap, warm socks, insulated underwear, insulated/hiking boots)
- Rain jacket, rubber boots (good for most areas).
- Breathable clothing for hot and muggy conditions.
- Sewing supplies (needle and thread, fabric, buttons, zippers for repairs).
- Hiking boots/work boots/Army boots.

Glasses, Contacts, and Hearing Aids

- Additional glasses, contacts.
- Magnifying glass.
- Hearing aids/sound amplification device; extra batteries.

Self-Defense and Safety

- Self-defense items (firearms, ammo, body armor).
- Alternative self-defense options besides a firearm (knife, baseball bat, golf club, hammer, hefty wrench, large flashlight, solid frying pan, stun gun, pepper spray, pepper ball gun, and Taser).
- Disorientation devices (very bright flashlights, strobe lights, lasers in the eye, flashbangs, or personal alarm).
- Motion-activated outdoor lights.
- Noisy dog breeds.
- Exterior door security (install long-throw deadbolts, upgrade strike plates, replace door jamb molding, add secondary locks/chains, and

replace door hinge screws with three-inch long wood screws).

- Extra door security (bar, wedge, or barricade).
- Window security film or plywood to board up ground floor windows.
- Fire escape ladder for second-story egress, if necessary.

PART 2: Items to Aid Your Survival Until Society Stabilizes

Lighting

- Battery-powered lanterns; appropriate batteries.
- Flashlights, several; appropriate batteries.

Refrigeration and Canning Equipment

- Chest freezer and/or mini fridge.
- Home canning equipment (water bath canner, pressure canner, jars of different sizes, lids, bands, recipe book); alternatives include dehydrating and freeze-drying.

Air Conditioning and Heating

- Box fans.
- Window screen material (including spline and roller tool).
- Blackout curtains, dark window tint, or aluminum foil for troublesome windows.
- Radiant heat barrier for the attic.

- Sleeping bags for each person (three-season or cold-weather).
- Seasoned firewood.
- Portable propane or kerosene heater (preferred), extra mantle/wicks.
- Fuel storage containers, filled.
- Electric blanket or heating pads.
- Bubble wrap to insulate windows.
- Reflective foil insulation to insulate a small room.
- Hand warmers.

Water

- 55-gallon water barrels and/or IBC totes.
- Plastic containers/bins for three-bin dishwashing method (will need bleach for sanitation bin).
- Laundry items (washboard or Wonderwash, clothesline or rack, clothespins, Fels-Naptha).
- Berkey water filter system and extra Black Berkey filters.
- Sawyer mini filter; consider making a gravity filter.
- Funnels of varying sizes.
- Water barrel pump or siphon hose (if you opt for rain barrels).

Waste Disposal

- Drain flood guard/mainline backflow prevention device (consult a plumber).
- Bucket toilet seat(s).

Stoves and Cooking

- Smoke alarms for each floor, bedrooms, kitchen, garage.
- Carbon monoxide detector for each floor.
- Fire extinguishers, ABC-style.
- Solar oven; consider making your own.
- WAPI indicator (for pasteurization only).
- Cast iron cookware, especially a Dutch oven, and lid lifter.
- Fire-starting supplies (matches, lighters, lighter fluid, ferro rod, or magnesium fire starter).
- Sterno cans or other canned fuel.
- Paper goods (paper plates, paper bowls, napkins).

Entertainment

- Deck of cards.
- Board games.
- Fiction books.
- Multi-game set.

Manual Tools

- Basic hand tools (hammer, handsaw, hacksaw, pliers, screwdrivers, tin snips); see Appendix C for a complete list.
- Basic power tools and related supplies (hand drill and drill bit set, circular saw, reciprocating saw); a manual hand drill may be useful.

- Personal safety protection equipment (safety glasses, ear protection, work gloves, hard hat, respirator).
- Gardening tools (round and flat shovels, scoop, spade, rake, hoe, mattock, handheld shovels, wheelbarrow or garden cart, scythe or billhook).
- Woodworking tools (axe, hatchet, splitting maul, wood splitting wedge, file set); may want to include additional handles and file set.
- Construction/demolition tools (hand auger, post hole digger, sledgehammer, ripping bar).
- Sundries (nails, screws, nuts, bolts, duct tape, glues, epoxy, caulking, foam insulation, lubricants, Vaseline).
- Home repair supplies (electrical wiring, copper pipe, PVC pipe, PEX tubing, plywood, lumber).

Tarps and Buckets

- Tarps, 6'x8', 8'x10' or 10'x12' sizes.
- Cordage to string up tarps and for other uses.
- Plastic sheeting is an alternative to tarps, but has better uses.
- Buckets, in five- or six-gallon sizes; consider food-grade buckets if you have a specific need.

Books

- Books for survival knowledge; see Appendix D for recommendations.

- Writing supplies (paper, pencils, pencil sharpener, erasers).
- Permanent markers, varying sizes.

Off-Grid Power

- Small solar setup including panels (and/or wind turbine), inverter, and batteries or solar generator and panels; pedal generator.

Miscellaneous Items to Stockpile

- Fishing gear (rod and reel, line, tackle).
- Pest control supplies for ants, cockroaches, spiders, flies; consider makeshift pest traps.
- Communications (shortwave radio, FRS radios).
- Fruit trees, berry bushes, vegetable seeds.
- Gas can, several.
- Fuel stabilizer (PRI-G for gasoline or PRI-D for diesel).
- Manual kitchen tools (can opener, egg beater, whisk, potato masher, and cheese grater).
- Knife sharpening set.
- Manual cleaning supplies (broom and dust pan, mop and bucket, scrub brushes, sponges, rags, manual carpet sweeper).
- Spare parts (spark plugs, air filters, belts/chains).
- Chemicals (engine oil, coolant, bar chain oil); specialty chemicals (penetrating oil, grease, lubes, etc.).

Appendix B: Food Storage Checklist

27 Grocery Store Foods to Stockpile

1. Breakfast cereals (fortified with fiber or vitamins; source of several macronutrients)
2. Canned beans (all types; good source of protein, fiber, and some vitamins)
3. Canned chili (alternative to soup; source of fiber)
4. Canned chowder (alternative to soup; source of fat)
5. Canned fish (all types; good source of protein and some vitamins and minerals)
6. Canned fruits (all types; major source of vitamins)
7. Canned meats (all types; good source of protein, carbs, and more)
8. Canned soups (all types; good way to mix a variety of nutritious foods)
9. Canned vegetables (all types; major source of vitamins)
10. Chocolates (required snack for many people; source of fat and calories)
11. Cookies (tasty snack; may include a variety of macronutrients)
12. Cooking oils, lard, butter (source of fiber, fat, calories)
13. Crackers (another snack; may be a good source of fat, fiber, and carbs)
14. Hard candies (all types; great for a carb boost and tasty treat for kids)

15. Ingredients to make bread (e.g., flour, salt, sugar, oil, yeast)
16. Iced tea (alternative drink; source of carbs)
17. Jelly (any kind; source of carbs)
18. Mayonnaise (will need refrigeration after opening; source of fat and calories)
19. Nuts and nut butters (raw is great, butters are good too; source of several macronutrients)
20. Pasta sauce (all types; needed for bulk spaghetti and macaroni)
21. Popcorn kernels (be sure to include cooking oil; source of fiber)
22. Potato chips (tasty snack; often a source of fiber, protein, and fat)
23. Pre-mixed canned drinks, such as V8 juice (alternative drink; includes vitamins)
24. Pretzels (tasty snack; source of carbs and fiber)
25. Seasonings (very useful to avoid appetite fatigue; stock plenty of options)
26. Seeds (raw is great and can be sprinkled in many meals; source of several macronutrients)
27. Sweetened powdered drink mix, such as lemonade or fruit drink (alternative drink)

11 Bulk Foods to Stockpile

1. Beans (black, pinto, great northern, and refried are all good to include)
2. Berry drink mix (to give you something sweet to drink)

3. Cocoa mix (another drink alternative)
4. Granola (for breakfast or even as a snack)
5. Macaroni (boxed macaroni would be an easier alternative for some meals)
6. Nonfat dry milk (for a variety of purposes)
7. Oats (regular is preferred, though instant oats would suffice)
8. Pancake mix (another great breakfast meal besides oats)
9. Potato flakes (not the instant potatoes; mashed potato mix would be an alternative)
10. Spaghetti (be sure to include pasta sauce)
11. White rice (brown rice could be stored instead, if you prefer)

19 Superfoods to Stockpile

1. Cacao powder (could be used for some baking needs, also as a chocolate drink; needs sweetened)
2. Chia seeds (bland taste can be sprinkled into almost anything)
3. Coconut oil (good fat to cook with)
4. Eggs (freeze-dried stores for years, real eggs can be coated in mineral oil to last months)
5. Flax seeds (includes similar nutrients to chia seeds, but higher oil content may not store as well)
6. Liquid minerals or multivitamin (more easily digested than a pill, useful during times of stress)

7. Multivitamin (pill form will stay viable the longest)
8. Protein powder (adequate amounts of protein is very important to maintaining a healthy body)
9. Spirulina (powder is a good choice and can go with almost any soup or stew)
10. Chlorella (like spirulina)
11. Wheat germ (bland taste can be sprinkled into almost anything)
12. Digestive enzymes (helps to breakdown foods; could be beneficial during times of stress)
13. Fiber powder or psyllium husk powder (helps keep you regular; stress can cause digestive problems)
14. Probiotics or water kefir grains (useful for proper gut health)
15. Vitamin C powder (avoid scurvy and boosts your immune system)
16. Apple cider vinegar (assorted health benefits as well as other possible uses)
17. Fish oil or omega 3 (assorted health benefits)
18. Green tea (or any tea you prefer, even teas that serve specific purposes)
19. Raw honey (nature's near perfect sweetener; lasts nearly forever)

Appendix C: Hand Tools Checklist

1. Dust Masks, several (preferably N-95 rated)
2. Safety Glasses
3. Ear Protection (e.g., ear plugs)
4. Leather Gloves, fitted
5. Larger Work Gloves
6. Chemical Gloves, heavy-duty preferred
7. Crosscut Hand Saw, 15"
8. Hacksaw (with extra blades)
9. Claw Hammer, 16 oz.
10. Crowbar, Wrecking Bar, 18"
11. Bolt Cutters, 14"
12. Folding Pruning Saw, 10"
13. Tin Snips / Aviation Snips
14. Utility Knife (with extra blades)
15. Manual Hand Drill
16. Drill Bit Set
17. Locking Pliers, large
18. Locking Pliers, small
19. Slip-Joint Pliers, large
20. Slip-Joint Pliers, small
21. Needle-Nose Pliers
22. Wire Cutters
23. Strap Wrench, small
24. Socket Set (with ¼-inch drive ratchet)
25. 1/4" Drive Ratchet (alternative to socket set)
26. Universal Socket (alternative to socket set)
27. Zip/Wire Ties, dozens (15" or similar length)

28. Bungee Cords, several (of different sizes)
29. 550 Paracord (25+ feet)
30. Velcro Strap (optional)
31. Staple Gun (with various staples sizes)
32. Quick-Release Clamps and/or spring clamps
33. Multi-Bit Screwdriver
34. Screwdriver Bit Set
35. Precision Screwdriver Set (optional)
36. Allen Wrench Set
37. Star Key Set
38. Carpenter's Framing Square, 12" x 6"
39. Metal File (for sharpening blade edges)
40. Cold Chisel
41. Torpedo Level
42. Tape Measure, 25' or longer
43. Mini Level (optional)
44. Razor Blade Scraper (with extra blades)
45. Wire Strippers
46. Mini Utility Bar, 7"
47. Nail Punch (optional)
48. Caulk Gun (with heavy-duty adhesive)
49. Gas Siphon (shaker hose)
50. Heavy-Duty Security Cable
51. Keyed Lock (to go with security cable)
52. Electrical Extension Cord (optional)
53. Pencils and Markers
54. Pencil Sharpener
55. Electrical Tape
56. Plumbers Teflon Tape
57. Bic Lighter

58. Duct Tape, roll
59. Magnetic Telescoping Pick Up Tool
60. Mirror, small
61. Magnifying Glass
62. Flashlight (with extra batteries)
63. Petroleum Jelly, small jar
64. J-B Weld (and/or strong glue)
65. 3-in-1 Household Oil
66. Nails (of varying sizes)
67. Other Sundries (screws, nuts and bolts, etc.)

Appendix D: Recommended Books

Food Storage and Cooking

- *Ball Complete Book of Home Preserving* by Judi Kingry
- *A Guide to Canning, Freezing, Curing & Smoking Meat, Fish & Game* by Wilbur F. Eastman
- *Root Cellaring: Natural Cold Storage of Fruits & Vegetables* by Mike Bubel
- *Seed Saving Bible* by Remo Gentry
- *Depression Era Recipes* by Patricia R Wagner
- *Clara's Kitchen: Wisdom, Memories, and Recipes from the Great Depression* by Clara Cannucciari

Long-Term Preparedness

- *The Encyclopedia of Country Living, 50th Anniversary Edition* by Carla Emery
- *Back to Basics* by Abigail Gehring
- *Prepper's Long-Term Survival Guide* by Jim Cobb
- *The Modern Survival Manual: Surviving the Economic Collapse* by Fernando "Ferfal" Aguirre
- *Storey's Guide to Raising Chickens, 4th Edition* by Gail Damerow
- *40 Projects for Building Your Backyard Homestead* by David Toht
- *The Backyard Homestead Guide to Raising Farm Animals* by Gail Damerow

Health and First Aid

- *The Survival Medicine Handbook, 4th Edition* by Dr. Joseph Alton
- *The Prepper's Medical Handbook* by William Forgey
- *Bushcraft First Aid: A Field Guide to Wilderness Emergency Care* by Dave Canterbury
- *Rosemary Gladstar's Medicinal Herbs* by Rosemary Gladstar

Self-Defense

- *Prepper's Home Defense* by Jim Cobb
- *Contact! A Tactical Manual for Post Collapse Survival* by Max Velocity

Survival Skills

- *Bushcraft 101* by Dave Canterbury
- *Advanced Bushcraft: An Expert Field Guide to the Art of Wilderness Survival* by Dave Canterbury
- *The Bushcraft Field Guide to Trapping, Gathering, and Cooking in the Wild* by Dave Canterbury
- *Edible Wild Plants: A North American Field Guide to Over 200 Natural Foods* by Thomas Elias

Miscellaneous

- *The Ultimate Book of Family Card Games* by Oliver Ho

- *The Knot Tying Bible: Climbing, Camping, Sailing, Fishing, Everyday* by Colin Jarman
- *DIY Natural Household Cleaners: How To Make Your Own Cleaners Naturally* by Matt Jabs
- *The Organically Clean Home: 150 Everyday Organic Cleaning Products You Can Make Yourself* by Becky Rapinchuk
- *Off Grid Solar Power Simplified* by Nick Seghers

Appendix E: List of Resources

Remember that all website links can be found here: https://rethinksurvival.com/books/sold-out-links.html

- Link 1: https://rethinksurvival.com/books/sold-out-checklist.php
- Link 2: https://rethinksurvival.com/kindle-books/sold-out-recommends/
- Link 3: https://providentliving.com/preparedness/food-storage/foodcalc/
- Link 4: https://www.calculator.net/calorie-calculator.html
- Link 5: https://providentliving.churchofjesuschrist.org/food-storage/home-storage-center-locations-map?lang=eng
- Link 6: https://rethinksurvival.com/kindle-books/food-storage-book/
- Link 7: https://survivalfreedom.com/can-you-freeze-canned-food-what-will-happen/
- Link 8: https://www.amazon.com/Shelf-Reliance-Pantry-Can-Organizers/dp/B07Q5GWVBQ/
- Link 9: https://www.thrivelife.com/variety-can-systems.html
- Link 10: https://keeperofthehome.org/homemade-all-natural-cleaning-recipes/

- Link 11: https://reason.com/2020/04/06/why-you-shouldnt-trust-anyone-who-claims-80-percent-of-americas-drugs-come-from-china/
- Link 12: https://www.wsj.com/articles/SB954201508530067326
- Link 13: https://www.amazon.com/Survival-Medicine-Handbook-Essential-Guide/dp/0988872501/
- Link 14: https://www.amazon.com/Preppers-Medical-Handbook-William-Forgey/dp/1493046942/
- Link 15: https://www.youtube.com/watch?v=ZaL4fLXXEJg
- Link 16: https://www.amazon.com/2022-Lippincott-Pocket-Guide-Nurses/dp/1975183223/
- Link 17: https://www.smithsonianmag.com/science-nature/here-are-reasons-you-shouldnt-take-fish-antibiotics-180964523/
- Link 18: https://jasemedical.com/
- Link 19: https://www.mayoclinic.org/healthy-lifestyle/nutrition-and-healthy-eating/in-depth/herbal-supplements/art-20046714
- Link 20: https://www.youtube.com/watch?v=AA46RP73EGo

- Link 21: https://www.youtube.com/watch?v=Z0udZGL9hqE
- Link 22: https://www.youtube.com/watch?v=Xfi12ljLNlw
- Link 23: https://www.youtube.com/watch?v=TWojdi-WkeU
- Link 24: https://www.forbes.com/sites/forbes-personal-shopper/2022/03/25/prescription-glasses-online-eyeglasses-online/
- Link 25: https://www.theseniorlist.com/hearing-aids/best/cheap/
- Link 26: https://www.webmd.com/healthy-aging/news/20170705/a-cheaper-alternative-to-hearing-aids#1
- Link 27: https://www.webmd.com/connect-to-care/lasik/does-insurance-cover-lasik-for-astigmatism
- Link 28: https://www.pewpewtactical.com/best-body-armor/
- Link 29: https://www.spartanarmorsystems.com/
- Link 30: https://www.ar500armor.com/
- Link 31: https://www.amazon.com/s?k=battery+powered+lantern
- Link 32: https://www.amazon.com/s?k=led+flashlight

- Link 33: https://www.amazon.com/Betgod-Flashlights-Flashlight-Resistant-Emergency/dp/B097DPZ2CL/
- Link 34: https://www.amazon.com/led-flashlight-high-lumens/dp/B07FNRNC2B/
- Link 35: https://www.amazon.com/AmazonBasics-Performance-Alkaline-Batteries-20-Pack/dp/B01B8R6PF2/
- Link 36: https://www.amazon.com/Panasonic-BK-3MCCA16FA-eneloop-Pre-Charged-Rechargeable/dp/B00JHKSN4O/
- Link 37: https://www.amazon.com/gp/product/B000LQMKDS/
- Link 38: https://www.amazon.com/Solar-AA-AAA-Rechargeable-Batteries/dp/B07SC9F73V/
- Link 39: https://www.amazon.com/MaximalPower-FC999-Universal-Alkaline-Batteries/dp/B008467K1E/
- Link 40: https://www.amazon.com/CYS-EXCEL-Hurricane-Candleholders-Cylinder/dp/B07MG86QGP/
- Link 41: https://www.amazon.com/Coleman-Premium-Dual-Fuel-Camping-Lantern/dp/B0009PURIQ/
- Link 42: https://www.youtube.com/watch?v=tsIcKCiotLY

- Link 43: https://www.foodsafety.gov/food-safety-charts/food-safety-during-power-outage
- Link 44: https://www.youtube.com/watch?v=aLM6rWmQxic
- Link 45: https://www.amazon.com/Root-Cellaring-Natural-Storage-Vegetables/dp/0882667033/
- Link 46: https://www.amazon.com/Ball-Complete-Book-Home-Preserving/dp/0778801314/
- Link 47: https://www.amazon.com/Ball-Including-Chrome-Plated-4-Piece-Utensil/dp/B00212IHBY
- Link 48: https://www.amazon.com/All-American-2-Quart-Pressure-Cooker/dp/B00004S88Z/
- Link 49: https://www.youtube.com/watch?v=4bLixQKH8BQ
- Link 50: https://www.amazon.com/Excalibur-3926TB-Dehydrator-Temperature-Dehydration/dp/B008OV4FD0/
- Link 51: https://www.dehydrate2store.com/
- Link 52: https://harvestright.com/
- Link 53: https://www.amazon.com/Machine-Presets-Delicate-Starter-Compact/dp/B08BRN1B7Q/

- Link 54: https://www.amazon.com/FoodSaver-FCARWJAH-000-Wide-Mouth-Regular-Accessory/dp/B016OL1AB6/
- Link 55: https://www.usaemergencysupply.com/information-center/packing-your-own-food-storage/oxygen-absorbers-recommended-amounts
- Link 56: https://www.popsci.com/keep-cool-minimal-ac/
- Link 57: https://www.chron.com/homes/article/Understanding-how-heat-enters-your-house-1539014.php
- Link 58: https://goroof1.com/2012/07/17/dark-shingles-make-house-hotter-2/
- Link 59: https://marmottenergies.com/much-sun-heat-house/
- Link 60: https://www.amazon.com/Melt-Candle-Company-Fire-Starter/dp/B084KK5P7G/
- Link 61: https://www.amazon.com/Dyna-Glo-WK24BK-Indoor-Kerosene-Convection/dp/B07JMF9JGY/
- Link 62: https://www.youtube.com/watch?v=fwCz8Ris79g
- Link 63: https://www.youtube.com/watch?v=dOwlOsCzOmk

- Link 64: https://www.amazon.com/MWS-Reflective-Insulation-Thermal-Barrier/dp/B07DHX8BPZ/
- Link 65: https://www.aquasana.com/info/average-water-usage-in-the-united-states-pd.html
- Link 66: https://www.waterrf.org/
- Link 67: https://www.cleanwateraction.org/features/harmful-algal-outbreaks-and-drinking-water
- Link 68: https://troopleader.scouting.org/information-camping/
- Link 69: https://www.amazon.com/5-Pack-Commercial-Plastic-Storage-Handles/dp/B094NB9XYN/
- Link 70: https://www.amazon.com/Columbus-Washboard-2072-Family-Silver/dp/B0000CBILJ/
- Link 71: https://www.amazon.com/Laundry-Alternative-Wonderwash-Retro-Colors/dp/B07FTVRV6P/
- Link 72: https://www.amazon.com/Berkey-Gravity-Fed-Filter-Purification-Elements/dp/B00CYW3EVO/
- Link 73: https://www.amazon.com/Sawyer-Products-SP128-Filtration-System/dp/B00FA2RLX2/

- Link 74: https://www.highwaterfilters.com/products/bucket-conversion-kit-for-sawyer-squeeze
- Link 75: https://www.youtube.com/watch?v=0KeLHMUfEtY
- Link 76: https://www.youtube.com/watch?v=N62RYVeW6y4
- Link 77: https://www.youtube.com/watch?v=jWjH9Ltxw_I
- Link 78: https://www.amazon.com/Emergency-Disaster-55-Gallon-Barrel-Drinking/dp/B00S6Z8UM6
- Link 79: https://www.amazon.com/Wadoy-Siphon-Transfer-Priming-Shaker/dp/B07C5RVT4W/
- Link 80: https://www.amazon.com/s?k=flood+guard
- Link 81: https://www.youtube.com/watch?v=ywYPNmwI2j4
- Link 82: https://www.youtube.com/watch?v=blX2ss5Fe2I
- Link 83: https://www.amazon.com/Container-Distributing-Emergency-Bucket-Toilet/dp/B0881Y9F3b/

- Link 84: https://www.youtube.com/watch?v=UBZzu0xobY8
- Link 85: https://www.amazon.com/Kidde-Monoxide-Detector-AC-Plug-Replacement/dp/B00M48BH30/
- Link 86: https://www.youtube.com/watch?v=bmAP4kv5O8c
- Link 87: https://rethinksurvival.com/8-simple-and-easy-rocket-stoves/
- Link 88: https://www.amazon.com/Multi-Fuel-Water-Pasteurization-Indicator-WAPI/dp/B009H5DT84
- Link 89: https://www.sunoven.com/all-american-sun-oven/
- Link 90: https://solarcooking.fandom.com/wiki/Category:Solar_cooker_plans
- Link 91: https://www.amazon.com/Lodge-L10DCO3-Dutch-Pre-Seasoned-5-Quart/dp/B004W4TXZI/
- Link 92: https://www.amazon.com/Lodge-Lifter-Lifting-Carrying-Ovens/dp/B0000TPDJE/
- Link 93: https://www.amazon.com/Ultimate-Book-Family-Card-Games/dp/1402750412/
- Link 94: https://www.amazon.com/Board-Game-Set-Wood-accented-Backgammon/dp/B002TLUZFS/

- Link 95: https://www.amazon.com/Swpeet-Powerful-Capacity-Pinions-Plastics/dp/B0773KZ35J/
- Link 96: https://www.youtube.com/watch?v=10k-DPcLrHU
- Link 97: https://rethinksurvival.com/net-guide/
- Link 98: https://seasonedcitizenprepper.com/preparedness-downloads/
- Link 99: https://www.mobile-solarpower.com/
- Link 100: https://windandsolar.com/
- Link 101: https://www.discoverboating.com/resources/best-fishing-apps
- Link 102: https://www.youtube.com/watch?v=nO4gGJ7mDO8
- Link 103: https://www.amazon.com/Seed-Saving-Bible-Vegetables-Fruits/dp/B0BB5KXLYY/
- Link 104: https://nasdonline.org/917/d000760/storing-gasoline-and-other-flammables.html
- Link 105: https://rethinksurvival.com/kindle-books/small-space-prepping-book/
- Link 106: https://rethinksurvival.com/kindle-books/

- Link 107: https://rethinksurvival.com/books/new-survival-books.php
- Link 108: https://rethinksurvival.com/kindle-books/collapse-survival-book/

Made in the USA
Columbia, SC
27 March 2023

14388881R00091